SKIN TRADE

Ann duCille

Harvard University Press
Cambridge, Massachusetts
London, England
1996

Library of Congress Cataloging-in-Publication Data
DuCille, Ann.
    Skin trade : Ann duCille.
        p. cm.
    Includes bibliographical references and index.
    ISBN 0-674-81081-3 (alk. paper) (cloth)
    ISBN 0-674-81084-8 (paper)
    1. United States—Race relations.   2. Marketing—Social aspects—United States.
    3. Popular culture—United States.   I. Title.
E185.615.D78 1996
305.8′00973—dc20   96-16061
CIP

For my younger brother Danny and in memory of my older brother Adrian Jr. (1945–1991), my first and best playmates

Acknowledgments

I have become fond of saying that my research on such public phenomena as Barbie and O.J. Simpson has made me suspect among my colleagues, who worry that some kind of mental breakdown has left me mindlessly playing with dolls and reading the *National Enquirer.* It is only a pleasantry, and nothing could be further from the truth. Wesleyan University provided an intellectually fertile environment where I was well supported in all of my work. No projects, however, generated more interest than my forays into the valley of the dolls and the "mountains of evidence." I am deeply indebted to colleagues, students, friends, family, and even strangers for the clippings, articles, faxes, and e-mail messages that helped to keep me abreast of my subjects. I particularly want to thank Joe and Kit Reed, Nancy Armstrong, Len Tennenhouse, Elizabeth Weed, Greta Slobin, Bill Stowe, Karen Bock, Cashman Prince, and Bill Burkhart, who were among the first to see that Barbie was not just an aberration—a pink blemish on my scholarly record. Erness Brody, Jennifer Brody, and Dianne Kelly shared their doll-collecting expertise with me; Farah Griffin, Sharon Holland, Amy Hundley, Chanda Bailey, and many others shared their doll stories. Marge Thomas kept me supplied with miniature McDonald's Barbies, and Jennifer Kirk and others at Atticus Books were ever on the alert for Barbie- and Simpson-related publications. Ellen Rooney read an earlier version of the Barbie essay and asked tough questions that challenged me to probe deeper. Phyllis Rose's insightful comments helped me finally put Barbie to bed. Charles Rowell pushed me to write about the Simpson case when I was convinced that there was at once too much to say and no way to say it. Late-night telephone conversations with Deborah McDowell about the Simpson trial, the Oklahoma City bombing, the academy, and life in general fed my mind and soul. Indira Karamcheti read several drafts and kept me thinking, writing, and laughing. My debt to her is inestimable.

I also would like to thank Jacqueline Urla, Mimi Nichter, Anne Fausto Sterling, and especially Mel McCombie, all of whom generously shared their research with me. Mel's interest in and knowledge of Barbie fed and encouraged my own. I am especially grateful to Patricia Williams, both for the inspiration of her own writing and for her generous support of my work. Special thanks are extended as well to Ben Jackson, Laura Santigian, Georgie Leone, and Werner Sollors for their friendship and encouragement, and to my editor, Lindsay Waters, whose faith in my work made this book possible. Others at Harvard University Press to whom I am indebted include Alison Kent, Joyce Backman, and Camille Smith. My final words of gratitude are to my family for their unwavering support and affection.

My chapters on Barbie and on the O.J. Simpson case were written specifically for this book. My work on so-called ethnic Barbie dolls began with an article entitled "Dyes and Dolls: Multicultural Barbie and the Merchandising of Difference," published in *differences* 6 (Spring 1994), from which one chapter draws. Chapter 2 was first published as "Phallusies of Interpretation: Engendering the Black Critical 'I'" in *Callaloo* 16 (Summer 1993); reprinted by permission of The John Hopkins University Press. Chapter 3, "The Occult of True Black Womanhood," first appeared in *Signs* 19 (Spring 1993), published by the University of Chicago Press; copyright ©1994 by the University of Chicago; all rights reserved. Both these chapters have been revised for this book. Chapter 4, on "Postcoloniality and Afrocentricity" is an expanded version of an essay originally published in *The Black Columbiad: Defining Moments in African American Literature and Culture* (Harvard University Press, 1994), edited by Werner Sollors and Maria Diedrich.

Contents

Capitalism feels good. Money feels good. Houses feel good. All that feels good, and it can be a complete substitution for *being* good. It's how we function in this country, and it's how we stimulate progress and change. Capitalism isn't necessarily bad in and of itself. But when it becomes a substitute way of living in the world, it can be so seductive that you end up on a journey of quenching a thirst that can never be satisfied.

—Toni Morrison, interview in *Essence* (May 1995)

Prologue

What You Mean "We," Kemo Sabe?

We hold these truths to be self-evident, that all men are created equal . . . We the people of the United States, in order to form a more perfect union . . . United we stand, divided we fall, and if our backs should ever be against the wall . . . Good fences make good neighbors . . . Where we walk to school each day / Indian children used to play / All about our native land / Where the shops and houses stand / Not a church and not a steeple / Only woods and Indian . . . People make the world go . . . Rally round the flag, boys . . . Give me your tired, your poor, your huddled masses yearning to breathe . . . Free at last, free at last. Thank God Almighty, we're free at last . . . And the last shall be first . . . I hear America singing . . . It's summer, the darkies are gay . . .

Even as intellectuals and politicians posit the declining significance of race, "racial difference" remains America's preeminent national narrative. It may defy definition; it may exist only in the minds of maddening (if not mad) scientists and Social Darwinists; it may be an empty category, a slippery concept,[1] a social construction, a trope. But whatever it is, race not only matters in the United States, it also has become—as in the days of slavery—both a commercial dividend and a continental divide.

From Uncle Ben's rice and Aunt Jemima pancakes (now pitched by the black singer Gladys Knight) to Benetton's multi-

1

million-dollar "United Colours" advertising campaign, J. C. Penney's "Afrocentric" mailorder catalog, Mattel's line of ethnic Barbie dolls, and a new breed of black "public intellectuals," race and its kissing cousin ethnicity have become precious commodities for both capitalism and the academy. Where race intersects with gender, class, and sex, its market value climbs even higher. Add murder, as in the O. J. Simpson case, and race becomes not only the "hottest property in America" but also "the greatest show on earth."[2]

Despite the ease with which the pronoun "we" has slipped from the lips of politicians and poets alike, the United States has never had an easy time living up to its professed plurality. The faces of racial and cultural diversity have spelled profit for big business, but the facts of racial difference—millions of real bodies—have spelled problems for the national enterprise. As the American melting pot has boiled over with immigrants from Mexico, Latin America, Asia, and the Caribbean, the American pie of prosperity has grown smaller—eaten away by too many mouths to feed, on the one hand, and by economic recessions, on the other. If this were indeed a land of plenty where the living is easy for everyone, white nationalists would probably care less about the approximately 18 million, mostly "colored" immigrants who have come to these shores since 1965. But in the face of rising costs and diminished opportunities, racial and ethnic differences threaten again to split the nation in two. And no matter how the socioeconomic divide is represented by conservatives and liberals—no matter whether the issue is welfare, education, employment, or affirmative action—the uncivil war of the 1990s is first and foremost a battle over entitlement: who gets to claim America, who gets to be American?

According to Speaker of the House Newt Gingrich: "To be an American is to embrace a set of values and living habits that have flourished on this continent for nearly four hundred years. Virtually anyone can become American simply by learning the ideas and habits of being an American." To prove his point, Gingrich summons up Henry Kissinger and Arnold

Schwarzenegger. "It's clear from their accents that they started somewhere else," he tells us, "but it is equally clear from their attitudes and behavior that they have become Americans."[3] It is significant that the two individuals Gingrich points out are white European men. It is also significant that the congressman's version of American history as a "series of romantic folktales that just happen to be true" either glosses over or completely ignores the near annihilation of the indigenous inhabitants of the Americas, the enslavement of Africans, the displacement and dispossession of Mexicans, the exclusion of the Chinese, and the internment of the Japanese.

Ironically, Gingrich praises Thomas Jefferson for his "God-is-just / justice-cannot-sleep-forever" antislavery rhetoric, without mentioning that Jefferson himself owned—and may have fathered—slaves. Nor does he mention that Jefferson wrote eloquently and often of the intellectual, physiological, and moral inferiority of blacks. "The first difference which strikes us is that of colour," he wrote in *Notes on the State of Virginia* (1782). "And is this difference of no importance? Is it not the foundation of a greater or less share of beauty in the two races?"[4] Concerned with much more than beauty, Jefferson went on to detail precisely how important this difference in color is as the visible sign of innate distinctions between the races:

> They secrete less by the kidneys, and more by the glands of the skin, which gives them a very strong and disagreeable odour . . . They are more ardent after their females: but love seems with them to be more an eager desire, than a tender delicate mixture of sentiment and sensation . . . in memory they are equal to the whites; in reason much inferior . . . in imagination they are dull, tasteless, and anomalous.

In each instance (except memory), it is blacks whom Jefferson found wanting, whom he judged inferior.

Jefferson may have preached that "commerce between master and slave is despotism," as Gingrich observes, also quoting from *Notes on Virginia,* but as a practicing slaveholder he continued to profit from that commerce. And though in theory he supported the eventual emancipation of slaves, he saw no future for free blacks in America and recommended that once manumitted they all be shipped (for their own good and for the good of the nation) back to Africa. "For if a slave can have a country in this world," he argued, "it must be any other in preference to that in which he is born to live and labour for another." Not only did Jefferson not see blacks as Americans, his own words suggest that he barely saw them as human. Perhaps this is why he saw no contradiction in declaring that all men are created equal and entitled to life, liberty, and the pursuit of happiness, even while he himself owned slaves and while his own pursuit of happiness depended on slave labor.

Most if not all of the racial stereotypes that have been assigned to African Americans for the past 350 years—from laziness and mental deficiency to hypersensuality and sexual deviance—can be found in *Notes on the State of Virginia.* Yet, given his time and place in history, Jefferson's bigotry is hardly remarkable. What is remarkable is the fact that Newt Gingrich leaves Jefferson's racism unremarked. Drawing from the same notoriously racist tract from which I have quoted, Gingrich reads right past the author's white-supremacist rhetoric and extracts from the text only those few phrases which would confirm Jefferson in the role of God-fearing, slavery-hating founding father and model American. My mentioning of Jefferson's racism and the alternative histories of *othered* Americans would be, in the Speaker's view, an un-American activity—just another example of "the querulous whining and petty grievances of so many modern columnists and academics."[5] "Up until the mid-1960s children and immigrants alike were taught how to be American," Gingrich writes, lamenting the loss of prayer, the Pledge of Allegiance, and the singing of "The Star-Spangled Banner" in public schools. Like many conservatives, he blames these losses and what he sees as the resultant decline of American civilization on the turn toward multiculturalism.

"Multiculturalism," he argues, "switched the emphasis from proclaiming allegiance to the common culture to proclaiming the virtues (real or imagined) of a particular ethnicity, sect, or tribe."

"Race" is curiously absent from Gingrich's reductive reading of multiculturalism as ethnic, sectarian, or tribal chauvinism. For the racially marked—black people in particular—simple assimilation into the common culture, into the "We the people of the United States," has never been merely a matter of how they talk, how they pray, how fervently they pledge allegiance to the flag, or even how patriotically correct they behave. For them—for what Langston Hughes called "the darker brother"—singing America, becoming American, has instead been finely connected to how they look, to the color of their skin. Nothing bears out this claim quite so completely as the would-be colorblind Constitution itself, which at various moments in history has denied or has been used to deny U.S. citizenship to African and Asian Americans, solely because they were not "white" in the sense intended by the same founding fathers whose legacy of institutionalized racism and sexism Gingrich thinks it is our patriotic duty to ignore. "America must be described in romantic terms," he writes. "To take the romance out of America is to de-Americanize our own country."

In practical terms, past injustices are far less relevant than present policy, and realism is far more useful than romance. A "Contract with America" that romanticizes a glorious past, while blaming welfare and disintegrating family values for the social problems of the present—unemployment, poverty, crime, drugs, teenage pregnancy—effectively denies the role that institutionalized racism continues to play in the decline of the inner city and the nation more generally. The welfare system, for example, is blamed for fostering a culture of poverty and a climate of indolence—for producing masses of men and women unwilling to work because the State will take care of them and their children. Recent studies suggest, however, that race or, more precisely, skin color remains a critical determinant of one's ability to earn a living wage and to support a family. This is particularly true in the inner city, especially for black men. Not only are white men eminently more employable than blacks of similar education and background, but light-skinned blacks have a better chance in the job market than their darker brothers. A study of two thousand able-bodied men in the Los Angeles area found that being African American and dark reduced the odds of working by 52 percent. According to the study, "light-skinned African-American men were more likely than their dark-skinned counterparts to be working, although their unemployment rate (20 per cent) was still high compared with that of white males."[6]

It hardly counts as evidence of anything, yet, as I stack these statistics against the Speaker's romantic notion that almost anybody can become American and succeed in America, I cannot help thinking of the perhaps tasteless but popular joke among blacks that immigrants become truly American at the precise moment that they learn how to say "nigger." It seems ironic (but in keeping with the national romance of colorblindness and racial equality) that throughout the media spectacle known as *The People v. Orenthal James Simpson*, the quintessentially American word "nigger" was recreated in the public imagination as the unspeakable thing never spoken—a word so extraordinary, so far outside common usage, so rabidly racist and un-American that it could only be alluded to as the "N word." He who would say "nigger" would also plant evidence to frame an innocent black man.

"Nigger" may have gone undercover in mixed company—as in the coded message "kill ALL ni gg ERS," which five white high school seniors in Greenwich, Connecticut, managed to slip into their yearbook in the spring of 1995.[7] It may have become publicly unspeakable, in polite company anyway, but the word and the racial animus associated with it remain very much alive in America, as much a part of what America is as the values and living habits Newt Gingrich champions. The failure to "fix" race relations in the United States may be directly related to our failure, on a national level, to confront how seriously and perhaps irreparably broken those relations are—how unremarkable the word "nigger" is, and the seething culture of resentment behind it.

In this book I explore the link between race and cultural commodification, between what liberals call cultural pluralism and what conservatives have dubbed political correctness, between feminist texts and masculinist readings, between the high theory of the academy and the popular culture of "the people." In different ways, each chapter examines both the meaning and the merchandising of race and gender in contemporary society. Taken together, they also interrogate the assumptions of Americanism, Afrocentrism, multiculturalism, and feminism. How does the notion of colorblind equality fit with the social and economic realities of black Americans? How does the idea of America as a "common culture" correspond with the way that our commodity culture uses race, gender, and sex not only to sell merchandise but also to sell particular products to particular communities? How is the commodification of alterity—the selling and buying of difference—manifested in the academy through what one might call an intellectual skin trade? What role do the mass media play in the production and marketing of race, gender, and culture?

1

Toy Theory: Black Barbie and the Deep Play of Difference

This is my doll story (because every black journalist who writes about race gets around to it sometime). Back when I started playing with Barbie, there were no Christies (Barbie's black friend, born in 1968) or black Barbies (born in 1980, brown plastic poured into blond Barbie's mold). I had two blonds, which I bought with Christmas money from girls at school. I cut off their hair and dressed them in African-print fabric . . . After an "incident" at school (where all of the girls looked like Barbie and none of them looked like me), I galloped down our stairs with one Barbie, her blond head hitting each spoke of the banister . . . until her head popped off, lost to the graveyard behind the stairwell. Then I tore off each limb, and sat on the stairs for a long time twirling the torso like a baton.

—Lisa Jones, *Village Voice*

Black Like Me

I was born in 1949, ten years before Barbie, who was not a part of my childhood. Though I did play with other dolls, my earliest memories of toys and games are of playing war with my two brothers. Growing up in the fifties, in the shadow of the second world war and the Korean conflict, I suppose it was natural for

It may be that my childhood recollections are inflected by adult perceptions, but I think that my mother's history—even with its triumphs—taught me subtle lessons about power relations. My mother was never a victim to me; she was invincible. Still, I learned from listening between the lines of her life that she was also vulnerable, in a way that was somehow connected to her color and her sex. It is no wonder that the white male body of an imaginary Glenn Evans became for me as a black girl child a much safer space—a far more empowering persona—than my mother's vulnerable black female body. Given the white male supremacy of my own world, through Glenn Evans I could project myself into the productive black woman I was determined to be. Becoming successful was not only what I would do for my race; it was the revenge I as a powerful, famous, wealthy black woman would take on the Halyards, on the relatives who did not take my mother in when she was a seven-year-old child, and on my own white hometown. I would be the conquering-hero "native daughter" my mother was not allowed to be.

I don't remember exactly how old I was when I saw my first black doll, perhaps ten or eleven, but I do remember the pleasure that went with the discovery. It was a big doll, about the same size as Patty Play Pal, who was three feet tall. This black doll was the most beautiful toy I had ever seen. She belonged to an elderly black woman we went to visit in the city. It seemed to me profoundly unfair that an old lady should have such a doll, and visions of dollnapping danced in my head. I went home empty-handed, but having seen black beauty I was never again satisfied with Betsy Wetsy and Patty Play Pal. Shortly thereafter, I hung up my dolls forever.

I doubt that the black doll I found so desirable as a child was any more "ethnically correct"[9] than the black Barbie dolls I discuss in the following pages. Herein lies the rub that makes any critique so riddled with contradictions. It was no doubt the doll's pigment, its brown plastic skin, that made it attractive, familiar, "like me." But if its brown pigment made this doll black like me, I as a child was judging the doll's racial similitude by the same outward sign of difference by which I myself was being judged. This time, though, there was comfort in that judgment—in the doll's "black like me" familiarity—however manufactured it may have been. Mattel, Inc., maintains that its black Barbie dolls provide a similar sense of self-recognition for millions of black girls. Familiarity in this instance is said to breed not contempt but pleasure and self-esteem. But what notions of gender and race are inscribed in this soft sell, in the "like me" familiarity of these black dolls? What does it mean that the verisimilitude of these dolls is *essentially* skin-color deep?

It is precisely this quintessential sign of difference—skin color—that is most deeply put into play in the making and mass-marketing of black-like-me Barbie dolls. In my own doll story, "look like me" is a metaphor for race and cultural experience. Similarly, when Lisa Jones says in her doll story that "all of the girls looked like Barbie and none of them looked like me," like-Barbie and like-me are codes for white and black. Mattel in effect has broken the code and manufactured a response. For Lisa Jones and for me—both as the black girls we were and as the African American women we are—a wealth of social, cultural, and material conditions as well as phenotypical differences are bound up in "like me." For Mattel as a corporation, however, "like me" is a shallow simile, refracted through the pigment of the plastic of which its dolls are made.

What does it mean when similarity and difference—even allowing for the power of metaphor—are calculated according to a like-me or an unlike-me that is not only a code for race but a code for race as skin color? Just what are we saying when we claim that a doll does or does not look like me, does or does not look black? How does black look? How does woman look? What would make a doll look like a "natural woman"? What would make a doll look authentically African American or realistically Nigerian or genuinely Jamaican? What prescriptive ideals of blackness are inscribed in such claims of authenticity? What cultural stereotypes of womanhood are embedded in the production of Mattel's "real dolls"? My questions come not from any intrinsic interest in Barbie itself. Rather, they are impelled by a broader concern with theories of difference in contemporary cultural criticism and with representations of gender, race, class, and sexuality in popular culture. How do Barbie dolls construct meaning not simply for the millions of little girls who play with them or even for the thousands of adults who collect them, but also for an increasing number of feminist scholars and social critics who have begun to analyze these dolls as cultural artifacts?[10]

The fact that skin color and other "ethnic features"—broader noses, thicker lips, wider hips—are used by toymakers to denote blackness raises critical questions about how we manufacture difference. In particular, Mattel's claim that its Shani dolls—a line of black Barbie-like dolls introduced in 1991—are more authentically African American because of such features may bring us dangerously close to the scientific racism of the nineteenth and early twentieth centuries. Black Barbie, then, has implications that reach far beyond the toy world and dangerously close to home.

Basic Training

More than simple instruments of pleasure and amusement, toys and games play crucial roles in helping children to determine what is valuable in and around them. As elements of the rites and rituals of childhood, dolls, games, storybooks, fairytales, and comics assist children in the process of becoming, in the task of defining themselves in relation to the world around them. As marketed by Mattel, Inc., Barbie dolls in particular invite children to imagine themselves in the dolls' image, to transport themselves into a realm of beauty, glamour, fun, success, and conspicuous consumption. "Imagine appearing on magazine covers, starring in fashion shows, and going to Hollywood parties," one ad reads, "as you, Shani, Asha and Nichelle [black Barbie dolls] live your dreams of beauty and success, loving every marvelous minute!"

Person, persona, and personality, Barbie is marketed not simply as a doll, a toy, but as _ole model for girls."[11] In fact, one concept behind the doll was _ _on that its adult female form would help to teach little gir_ _ _come beautiful, feminine women—"just like Barbie," a _ _ll appears in advertising copy. Early Barbie dolls ca _ _ _ _ries such as bras, petticoats, girdles, and garters, which would guide little girls in negotiating these then-essential accouterments of womanhood and fashion.[12] In the words of Billyboy, a British fashion designer and Barbie doll aficionado, Barbie's undergarment sets of the fifties and early sixties symbolized adulthood for most girls. As such, they "allowed young women to anticipate the structured and difficult-to-wear undergarments of the era."[13]

Today, at a time when Madonna has transformed underwear into outerwear, Barbie also takes to the streets in such underclothes as see-through bustiers and spandex leggings. Whether for day or night, lingerie has made a comeback as popular accessories for Barbie dolls, which are generally sold without undergarments. (In 1995 Teacher Barbie's lack of underwear triggered consumer complaints that the doll seemed to be teaching something other than reading, writing, and arithmetic.) A line of lingerie introduced in 1991 as Barbie's "Fancy Frills" presents little girls—"5 and over"—with four sets of accessories in which to dress their dolls, including lacy, see-through teddies and satin bras and panties. Other lingerie sets on the market include a "Wedding Day" ensemble, blue satin panties and camisole with a matching bed jacket and high-heel pumps. The label on the package may say "Wedding Day," but the garments inside more readily suggest the wedding night.

While these ensembles are sold separately as accessories, some of the dolls come prepackaged with alternative nighttime wear. For example, Madison Avenue Barbie, a special F.A.O.

Schwarz limited-edition doll introduced in 1991, is dressed to the nines in a fashionable pink suit and stylish green trapeze coat, but what she's shopping for—what she carries in her Schwarz rocking-horse-emblazoned shopping bag—is no teddy bear but a hot-pink teddy, a sexy undergarment of the Victoria's Secret variety.

The contradiction of the toystore tote bag and the hot-pink teddy suggests the same blurring of the lines between innocent child's play and adult sexual fantasy that the Barbie doll itself suggests. The hot-pink teddy and similar garments not only teach little girls how to be grown up; they also prepare them for their role as adult consumers. But the messages that Barbie and her garments send are mixed and not just for or about little girls who would be women and shoppers. The elaborate lingerie ensembles, day-glow bustiers, lace panties, and lycra tights of the nineties teach more than dress, deportment, and consumption; they spell out the ABCs of sex and seduction.

Moreover, the narrative of sensuality underneath the doll's wardrobe is intertwined with the narrative of beauty and success that is the enabling script for Barbie's personal romance and commercial empire. As would-be toys for girls, then, Barbie and her intimate trappings represent a seemingly innocent space for the displacement of adult ambivalence about sexuality. Like any good fetish, Barbie at once absorbs our sins and absolves us of them. She transforms the unclean thoughts of grown-ups into the immaculate conceptions of children. Figured as mere child's play, Victoria's Secret is let out of the brown paper bag, as it were, and placed rocking-horse pure in the presexual space of the little girl's playroom.

There is still more to the story. The original (or, as it turns out, not so original) 1959 Barbie was modeled after a sexy, adult-bodied, German-made doll called "Bild Lilli." The Lilli doll, itself taken from a gold-digging comic-strip character, became a kind of sex toy, which reportedly was sold primarily to men in tobacco shops and other male haunts. Barbie's taste in clothes—or, rather, Mattel's—betrays the doll's European origins as erotica. In their U.S. incarnations, Barbie and her wardrobe reflect the American ideal of continental decadence and the degree to which that decadence—a "No, No, Nanette" naughtiness—is located in the female form.

Probing deeper, a Freudian interpretation might even uncover both repressed sexual desire and a kind of Paris envy. In Paris and throughout Europe, lingerie resonates with a certain *je-ne-sais-quoi,* which Americans have envied but never gotten quite right. In the European underwear world, distinctions are finely drawn between the decadent and the delicate. Barbie's intimate apparel, however, "blurs the boundary between the bordello and the boudoir,"[14] transporting into toyland a perhaps uniquely American confusion about sex, sin, and the body.

For Mattel, of course, any relationship between sex and the text of Barbie—especially the charge that sex sells Barbie—is a figment of the imaginations of dirty-minded adults, who project their own sexual preoccupations and perversions onto innocent toys intended for children. Whether a fashion model, a flight attendant, or an astronaut, Barbie, according to her manufacturer, has always been a fine, upstanding career girl (as opposed to the "working girl" her wardrobe may suggest). But the company's own marketing strategies and advertising copy would seem to contradict this plea of innocence, since the prose and pictures used to sell Barbie often sexualize the doll and position it as an object of both desire and emulation. An ad for a Barbie T-shirt, for example, shows a truncated (head and torso only) version of the doll—arms bent back and chest thrust forward—floating above a caption that reads: "Your Barbie doll will look hot in this cool T-shirt." In such ads—which replicate the calendar-girl and sex-kitten poses of adult models—both the graphics and the words invite an erotic gaze. Mattel also markets a line of "cool" career fashions for its Barbie dolls, but most of Barbie's wardrobe has more to do with the bedroom and the ballroom than with the boardroom. If Barbie is indeed a role model for girls, just what role is she modeling? Linked as they are to a master narrative of beauty, boys, and fun, fun, fun, these lingerie sets may teach little girls more about taking their clothes off than about putting them on.

This lesson is reinforced through hundreds of other components of Barbie culture—from video and board games, puzzles, and comic books to an exercise tape and a line of girls' clothing called Barbie for Girls. Board games such as "Barbie Dress Up," "Barbie Dream Date," and "Barbie Queen of the Prom," along with a new line of video games for Sega Genesis and Super Nintendo, all invite players to join Barbie in the happiness of her favorite pursuits: shopping, dressing up, dating, and having fun. "Barbie Fashion Designer," a CD-ROM computer game introduced in 1996, allows players to design Barbie clothes on the computer and print them on a light fabric that works in any printer. In "Barbie Magic Fairy Tales," another computer game still in the planning stage, Barbie as Rapunzel reportedly gets to rescue Prince Charming Ken from the spell of a wicked witch. The would-be heroic twist to this plot does not disguise the fact that in all of these games, winning or succeeding is synonymous with having the right looks, the right hair, the right clothes, and the right boyfriend.

The same messages are imparted by *Barbie, the Magazine for Girls,* a bimonthly fanzine aimed at girls roughly between the ages of four and twelve. Like the Miss America pageant, which bills itself as a scholarship program rather than a beauty contest, the Barbie magazine presents itself as educational rather than commercial. Any given issue might include a recipe for frozen fruit pops, a feature on outstanding American girls, or a math lesson that asks readers to use their arithmetic skills to assist Barbie on a shopping spree. ("Barbie is shopping for a new party dress. Read the clues below to figure out which dress she is going to buy.") What the magazine actually does, however, is sell Barbie. Child models—often striking adult poses replete with grown-up hairdos—are used to sell the doll and a variety of Barbie-related products. Ingeborg Majer O'Sickey argues in fact that the publication uses child-women models to sell highly particularized notions of beauty and femininity. Both the images and the editorial beauty guides function as a kind of "basic training" designed to lure little girls into the adult world of clothes, cosmetics, and consumption.[15]

It is exactly this indoctrination into a particular, fixed notion of femininity that concerns me: the role-model persona Barbie projects, along with the like-me correlative that Mattel uses to sell black versions of the doll. It is surely significant that these dolls, which once came only in white, are now mass-produced and mass-marketed to "look like" the racial other; to resemble the "like me" missing from my own childhood play; to represent the vast array of colors, races, ethnicities, and nationalities that make up the real world.

Bawdy Language

Like Madonna, Barbie has developed both a posse of devoted fans and a gang of hostile critics. For millions of children and adults in the United States and around the world, she is the most popular, most enduring of all toys—the doll that children and collectors most love to consume. For others—wary parents and feminist scholars in particular—Barbie is a dangerous weapon against womankind—the icon of idealized femininity they most love to hate or at least interrogate, deconstruct if not destruct. The doll's exaggerated proportions and the standard set by her morbidly thin form have been at the center of controversy. (If life-size, her measurements would be something like 36–18–33, depending on who's calculating, and she wouldn't have enough body fat to menstruate regularly.) Indeed, read by many as a metaphor for young women often described pathologically as empty-headed, self-absorbed, anorexic material girls, Barbie has long attracted the ire of feminists, who revile her as yet another manifestation of the damaging myths of female beauty and the feminine body that patriarchy thrusts upon girls and women.

But while Anna Quindlen and other feminists may want to drive a silver lamé stake through her plastic heart, Barbie has her feminist fans too, some of whom see her as a revolutionary doll whose professional roles have run ahead of the prevailing images of women as housewives, secretaries, and nurses.[16] "Barbie was an astronaut years before Sally Ride," one of the doll's defenders points out.[17] And though she toys with Ken, she is not dependent on him or any other man. In fact, Ken is little more than another accessory—like Barbie's lingerie or her condo or her Porsche. Not just an empty-headed, materialistic bimbo who finds math class tough,[18] Barbie is for some a feminist heroine who has been first in war (Desert Storm Barbie saw active duty in the Gulf), first in peace (Ambassador Barbie held her own summit in 1990), and always in the hearts of her people (Americans buy her at the rate of one doll every second).

It can also be argued that Barbie stands apart from other, more traditional dolls, whose place is in the home. Karen Sanchez-Eppler maintains that all dolls are intended to teach domesticity,[19] but Barbie's mission and methodology are far more complex than those of Betsy Wetsy and Tiny Tears. Those baby dolls invoked the maternal, as they and the bottles and diapers with which they were packaged invited little girls to nestle and nurture. Barbie's voluptuous adult form, on the other hand, summons not the maternal but the sexual—not the nurturant married mother but the sensuous single woman.

Her adult female form has made Barbie a titillating toy for many children, whose doll play is often sexual in nature.[20] But if her protruding plastic mounds signify simmering sensuality, what are we to make of the doll's missing genitalia? Some cultural critics read Barbie's genital ambiguity as "homage to 'good taste.'"[21] The doll's anatomically inaccurate form invites such readings, but Barbie's crotch is not simply ambiguous; it is missing—an absence, as Freud dubbed female genitalia in general. Whereas Ken and his black counterpart Jamal have bumps where the groin should be and simulated jockey shorts etched into the plastic,[22] most female Barbie dolls come neither with underpants nor with a hint of anything that needs covering. As an icon of femininity, Barbie is locked into a never-never land in which she must be forever sensual without the possibility of sex. Conspicuously sensual on top but definitively nonsexual below, her plastic body has inscribed within it the very contradictory whore/madonna messages with which patriarchy taunts and traumatizes young women.

The mixed messages of Barbie make criticism difficult. Whatever points she might get for her career ambitions are immediately countered by the unrelenting reminders of her essential femininity. Where Barbie is figured as an astronaut, she also comes with permanently arched feet to accommodate her signature stiletto heels—which if life-size would rise a painful five inches from the floor. Army Barbie comes dressed in fatigues, but her flat combat boots won't stay on her vaulted feet. Police Officer Barbie wears a blue uniform, but she doesn't pack a pistol or a nightstick or even a pair of handcuffs; what she packs is a gold and white chiffon party dress with matching pumps, presumably for dancing at the policeman's ball.[23] And Presidential Candidate Barbie (Mattel says she didn't win) comes with both a Nancy-Reagan-red business suit and a red, white, and blue inaugural ball gown.[24] The most recent manifestation of Dr. Barbie comes with a pink plastic stethoscope, a white lab coat, and blue spike heels to match her short blue dress. What's new with this edition, though, is the baby Dr. Barbie holds tucked under one arm—perhaps the most appropriate accessory for a real woman.

Yet, as lessons go, the endless reminders that Barbie is a woman seem inconsequential in the face of serious charges that the doll may be hazardous to the emotional and physical health of girls. Many recent surveys and studies have documented a preoccupation with dieting and an overall dissatisfaction with their bodies among adolescents.[25] Barbie dolls have been implicated in a number of these studies, including a report aired on *ABC Nightly News* in which the Barbie workout tape ("Dance! Workout with Barbie") was featured as an example of how far the mystique of beauty and thinness has permeated the world of children.[26]

Among adolescents—particularly white female adolescents—the mystique of thinness is being played out in a dieting epidemic. The anthropologists Mimi Nichter and Nancy Vuckovic of the University of Arizona have examined how this epidemic manifests itself in the speech of adolescents, through what the scholars call "fat talk." "I'm so fat" has become a refrain for a multitude of white, middle-class adolescent girls, most of whom are more likely to be underweight than overweight. Here too Barbie has been implicated. Nichter and Vuckovic report that the majority of their informants described the perfect girl as 5'7", 100–110 pounds, with a good figure, long blonde hair, and big blue eyes. "To many girls," they conclude, "the ideal girl is a living manifestation of the Barbie doll."[27]

The same study also suggests that African American female adolescents are markedly less preoccupied with weight and dieting than either their white or Hispanic peers. Black girls, the study concludes, generally have more flexible notions of beauty and tend to be more concerned with such issues as style, pride, and personality.[28] Though such findings might suggest less cause for concern about eating disorders among women of color, the feminist sociologist Becky Thompson has issued a warning against easy assumptions about the relation between race, class, culture, and eating patterns. "Since there is no such thing as a monolithic 'black community,'" she argues (or a monolithic "white middle class" or a generic woman, one might add), "any attempt to identify a single idea about weight, size, and food quickly breaks down."[29]

There can be little doubt that eating problems have a certain potency within and across races, ethnicities, classes, cultures, and sexual orientations. It is equally apparent that these disorders—from anorexia and bulimia to compulsive eating and obesity—are affected by a vast array of social forces, including racism, sexism, and homophobia, as well as by standards of beauty and health promoted by the diet, exercise, clothing, and cosmetic industries, not to mention the movies, the media, and the medical profession. But if white Barbie has helped to inspire the current dieting crisis—if the archetypal blond, blue-eyed Barbie doll is indeed a progenitor of eating disorders among white adolescents—will the current proliferation of black Barbie dolls have similar consequences for African American girls?

I ask this question somewhat tongue-in-cheek and Sara Lee cheesecake in hand. These are serious issues to be sure, but blaming Barbie for adolescent anorexia would be a little like blaming Sara Lee for obesity. Like eating problems, the beauty ideals that Barbie embodies have been around for generations, perhaps centuries. The doll's slight yet voluptuous frame melds into a single figure at least two different ideals of beauty, dating back to the Middle Ages and perhaps to the ancient Greeks and Egyptians: the lean, long form, on the one hand, and the curvaceous, full-bosomed body, on the other.

Even the preoccupation with excessive dieting is not unique to our time. More than a century ago, Harriet Beecher Stowe complained that Americans were too concerned with weight. According to Stowe and other nineteenth-century social critics, preference for a lean and hungry femininity among the genteel classes created such public pressure to be thin that "willowy girls" feared "nothing so much as growing stout."[30]

Although the white, willowy, small-waisted wisp of a girl has had a long run as the body beautiful in many circles, there have been moments when and regions where a pleasing plumpness has found favor. And "black is beautiful" has also had its moments of glory. Making a point about what she calls the "democratization of beauty," Lois Banner marks the 1960s as the moment when rigid standards of beauty were relaxed to such an extent that a "variety of racial and ethnic looks" could be viewed as attractive. "By the 1970s," Banner adds, "blacks and orientals (although in small numbers) even advanced to the finals of the Miss America pageant, while the Miss Universe contest presented as beautiful a worldwide selection of disparate faces and bodies."[31]

Since Banner's book was published in 1983, five black women have been crowned Miss America (Vanessa Williams in 1984; Suzette Charles, who completed Williams's disrupted reign; Debbye Turner in 1990; Marjorie Judith Vincent in 1991; and Kimberly Aiken in 1994).[32] But unless I have missed a few pageants along the way, the body types, the apparel, and the hairstyles of the black women crowned Miss America or of the colored women crowned Miss Universe have differed little from those of the white contestants. It is interesting to note, for example, that after being crowned Miss Universe in 1994, Sushmita Sen, Miss India, said that the best advice she received about the pageant was to wear a western dress rather than a sari for the evening-gown competition. What Banner describes as prized "racial and ethnic looks" have had more to do with hair, clothes, and style than with body type. And whatever moments of popularity and commercial cachet "ethnic looks" may have enjoyed, they have generally found favor among the radical and the rebellious. We have yet to see a black Miss America or a black Miss Universe with an Afro or cornrows or dreadlocks. As Banner herself later notes, the fact that "the commercial beauty culture presented blacks as beautiful does not mean that the popularity of traditional sorts of looks went out of style. Voluptuous blondes and elegant brunettes were still greatly admired."[33]

I am not convinced that the commercial beauty culture has ever presented black people as beautiful per se; instead capitalism has appropriated what it sees as certain signifiers of *blackness* and made them marketable. The distinction I make may be the difference between intrinsic value and external vogue. It's like the suntan phenomenon: many white women and men risk skin cancer to darken their pale flesh without seeing black—that is, black people—as beautiful. I have similar misgivings about the social significance of Banner's claims for the "continuing democratization of beauty." Barbra Streisand may have advanced to stardom without reducing the size of her nose, but the fact remains that nose jobs, facelifts, breast implants, tummy tucks, liposuction, and other forms of cosmetic surgery are on the rise, as more and more women (and men) set out in pursuit of what remain the dominant ideals of American beauty.

At the end of her study, Banner made a prophetic observation: "It is possible," she wrote in 1983, "that if the resurgent conservativism of the 1980s succeeds in its goal of re-creating domesticity as the dominant ideal for women, the empty-headed child-woman of the 1950s may re-emerge." Barbie, who is more popular now than ever before, may suggest not only a reemergence of conservativism but the endurance of particular cultural ideals of beauty and dominant stereotypes of women. Yet however great the temptation to make Barbie responsible for our beauty ideals, it is important to view this doll (and others like it) as more effect than cause. Certain traditional ideals of beauty and femininity operate so effectively in contemporary society because they are overdetermined by advertising, by the media, and by other technological and ideological elements of commodity culture. To posit Barbie as more effect than cause, however, is not to suggest that she is innocent or "just a doll," as Mattel conveniently maintains whenever its premium product is criticized. Barbie is both product and purveyor of many of the dominant white ideals of beauty. Not only does she project a decidedly thin but voluptuous body image, she also comes with instructions for becoming thin and beautiful like Barbie.

Barbie Baby Sits, a 1963–64 edition of the doll, came with a booklet called "How to Lose Weight." The advice was "don't eat." And Barbie's 1965 "Slumber Party" ensemble came with a bathroom scale set at 110 pounds. More recently, Barbie, if only by implication, has endorsed cosmetic surgery as a means of attaining the perfect body. The January-February 1994 issue of *Barbie Bazaar* includes a photo essay on the transformation of a doll called Happy—presumably Happy To Be Me, a doll made and marketed by a competitor of Mattel—into Happy To Be Midge, another Barbie-like doll made by Mattel. Within the pages of *Barbie Bazaar*, the transformation is accomplished through the wonders of plastic surgery performed by Dr. Ken Doll at the Cosmetic & Reconstructive Surgery Clinic of Atlanta.[34] The photo essay tracks "Poor Happy," who's "so unhappy," as she goes from a miserable doll living a "humdrum life in Woodbury, Minnesota," into a beautiful Barbie clone, off "to seek 'Fame and Fortune' in Hollywood."[35] "Midge tells Dr. Ken all about herself and her motivation for the surgery," the narrative informs us. "She points to a picture of Barbie on his office wall (left) and tells him that Barbie has the body she has always wanted." In order to achieve "the authentic Barbie look—extensive reconstructive surgery is needed." In the language of the narrative, "Happy is stretched, tightened, tucked here and there, and built up in all the right places. When the grueling surgery is completed, only Happy's hair remains the same."

Through both words and pictures (including photographs of the doll bandaged from head to toe after her radical surgery), Happy's pre-surgery misery is linked to her physical appearance, at the same time that her post-op joy and the promise of a glamorous life as a fashion model are linked to her becoming more like Barbie, to having achieved "the authentic Barbie look."

But to fully understand the implications of Happy's regeneration through the violence of head-to-toe plastic surgery, we should know that Happy To Be Me, which was introduced by High Self Esteem Toys in the late 1980s, was promoted as a doll whose more "realistic" proportions (36–27–38 if life-size) were supposed to help young girls develop healthier attitudes toward their own bodies. The idea of a fashion doll that operated outside the culture of thinness was a popular one among healthcare professionals, feminists, and paparazzi alike, and this new imperfect doll won endorsements from concerned parents and such heavy hitters as the National Association of Anorexia Nervosa and Associated Disorders.[36] Unfortunately, the doll itself was never as popular as its press. Today (or last I knew) the doll is all but defunct—available only through special orders, if at all. In M. G. Lord's inimitable words: "Mothers may have told reporters, 'Wow! A doll with hips and a waist,' but they bought Barbie."[37]

If the birth of Happy To Be Me was meant to send a positive message to adolescent girls about their own bodies, what kind of message does her death or, rather, her surgical transformation into beautiful Midge transmit to teenagers? But there may be another message embedded in Happy's story as well. Given her role as an alternative—if not an antidote—to Barbie, Happy To Be Me's failure in the marketplace may tell us something about ourselves as consumers and our relation to the beauty that is the beast of Barbie. This, then, may be the most telling doll story of all. Groucho Marx said he wouldn't want to belong to a club that would have him as a member. In the same vein, I'm not so sure that most of us really want to buy a doll that looks like us. We can criticize its unreality all we want, but perfect female beauty of the Barbie kind is a commodity we buy and buy and buy.

Susan Willis, a Marxist theorist, maintains that in late twentieth-century capitalism gendering is finely connected to commodity consumption. "When gender is assimilated to the commodity," she writes, "it is conceived as something fixed and frozen: a number of sexually defined attributes that denote either masculinity or femininity on the supermarket shelf of gender possibilities."[38] Barbie dolls represent a potent example of gender as commodity and femininity as something fixed and frozen in plastic. But race is also a hot commodity in late capitalism. What happens when gender as a commodity is fixed and frozen in plastic together with race as commodity?

Though Barbie is to me troubling in all of her manifestations—white as well as colored—I am particularly concerned with the many would-be multicultural versions of the doll that have appeared since 1980: Jamaican, Nigerian, and Kenyan Barbie; Malaysian, Chinese, and Indian Barbie; Mexican, Brazilian, Hawaiian, Eskimo, Japanese, and Native American Barbie, and on and on. As carbon copies of an already grossly stereotypical and fantastically female original, these colorized Mattel toys are a particularly useful site in which to explore the marketing of race and gender difference.

Play's the Thing

Nowhere in the toy world is the universalizing myopia of mass production more conspicuous than in the making, marketing, and consumption of Barbie dolls. By Mattel's reckoning, Barbie enjoys 100 percent brand name recognition among girls aged three to ten, 96 percent of whom own at least one doll, with most owning an average of eight. When Barbie turned thirty in 1989, *Newsweek* noted that nearly 500 million Barbies had been sold, along with 200 million G.I. Joes—"enough for every man, woman, and child in the United States and Europe."[39] Those figures increased dramatically over the next five years, bringing the worldwide Barbie population to 800 million by the time the doll turned thirty-five in 1994. In 1992 alone, a billion dollars' worth of Barbies and accessories were sold. The following year, Barbie dolls sold at an average of one million per week, with overall sales exceeding the $1 billion all-time high set the year before. As the *Boston Globe* reported on the occasion of Barbie's thirty-fifth birthday, nearly two Barbie dolls are sold every second somewhere in the world; about half of the dolls sold are purchased in the United States.[40]

Created by Ruth Handler, one of the founders of Mattel, and a team of designers and engineers (including a former aerospace engineer named Jack Ryan, who was once married to Zsa Zsa Gabor), Barbie dolls have been a real force in the toy market since they were first introduced at the American Toy Fair in 1959. In fact, despite the skepticism of toystore buyers—who at the time were primarily male—the first shipment of half a million dolls and a million costumes sold out immediately.[41]

Made, some maintain, not only in imitation of but from the same mold as the German Lilli doll, the first Barbie dolls were manufactured in Japan. Even though these white dolls sold well, Mattel reportedly discovered that many U.S. consumers—war with Japan and Korea still on their minds—were concerned that the doll's features were too "Oriental."[42] Mattel spokespersons and doll experts maintain that the alleged Asian cast of the original Barbie was an optical illusion that had more to do with the doll's face paint than with its actual design. Sharply tapered heavy black mascara gave the doll's eyes an "almond shape," which some have described as stereotypical Oriental.[43] Others maintain that their makeup made the original Barbie dolls look more European—more like Marlene Dietrich—than like the American girl next door. Although the face mold remained the same, these cosmetic accidents were quickly corrected in subsequent editions of the doll by changing the face paint: by softening the severely arched eyebrows and tinting the pupils what became a signature blue.

If any deviation from a white, all-American-girl look was a cosmetic accident in the original Barbie, Mattel in the late sixties and early seventies began producing what it marketed first as "colored," then as "black" versions of the doll. (Latina, Asian, and other ethnic dolls were added in the early 1980s.) Colored Francie, as the first black Barbie-like doll was called, premiered in 1967. Like white Francie Fairchild introduced the year before, Colored Francie was presumably Barbie's "MODern" younger cousin. As a white doll patterned in the image of Hollywood's Gidget and Britain's Twiggy, white Francie had been an international sensation, but Colored Francie was not destined to duplicate her prototype's success. The black-is-beautiful theme of the time may have suggested that there was a ready market for a beautiful black doll, but Colored Francie did not sell well.

Evelyn Burkhalter, owner of the Barbie Hall of Fame in Palo Alto, California—home to 16,000 Barbie dolls—attributes Colored Francie's commercial failure to the racial climate of the sixties. Doll-purchasing patterns, it seems, reflected the same resistance to integration that was felt elsewhere in the nation.

In her implied family ties to white Barbie, Colored Francie inadvertently suggested more than simple integration, however. She implied miscegenation: a make-believe mixing of races that may have jeopardized the doll's market value. Moreover, Francie Fairchild had an already well-established persona as a white teenager. Even the surname Fairchild spoke to her Caucasian identity. How was this fair child to share her name and persona with guess-who's-coming-to-dinner colored kin?

Other Barbie buffs have suggested that Colored Francie flopped because of her straight hair and Caucasian features.[44] Indeed, Mattel's first black doll was made from the same mold as white Francie, but less by design, it seems, than for expediency. Applauding Mattel for its concern for the black community and its efforts to help rebuild Los Angeles after the Watts riots of 1965, Kitturah Westenhauser writes:

> The urgency expressed by [black leaders] to unite the community in the healing process was linked with an effort by Mattel to market alongside the Barbie doll, a black friend. To typify the African-American features in a doll required new sculpting, castings, and refinement in all aspects of the doll's production. For Mattel, [the] challenge to accomplish the task of producing a doll was up against the deadline of the New York City Toy Fair of 1967. Time restraints would deny Mattel the marketing of a doll with uniquely African-American qualities by the close of 1966. The doll chosen to fill the void until further refinements could be made to the black ethnic mold was the Francie doll.[45]

After the Watts riots, Mattel did contribute valuable technical support and $150,000 of start-up capital to Shindana Toys, a division of Operation Bootstrap, a nonprofit black self-help organization in South Central Los Angeles.[46] But a less generous reading of the circumstances of Colored Francie's birth might argue that Mattel saw a marketing opportunity and rushed into the fray with an all-deliberate speed that integration otherwise lacked. Shindana means "competitor" in Kiswahili. Ironically, even as it helped launch Shindana Toys, Mattel also made itself the fledgling company's principal competitor by rushing its own black doll to market.[47]

Although the doll's white features may have played some role in its failure to win a following, it's likely that Mattel's decision to call its first black Barbie "Colored Francie" also contributed to the doll's demise. The use of the term "colored" in the midst of civil-rights and black-power activism suggested that, while Francie might be "MODern," Mattel was still in the dark ages. In any case, neither black nor white audiences bought the idea of Barbie's colored relations, and Mattel promptly took the doll off the market, replacing her with a black doll called Christie in 1968.

Christie, who was given her own black persona as Barbie's friend rather than as part of the family, sold well and remained on the market until 1985. Although a number of other black dolls appeared throughout the late sixties and seventies—including the Julia doll, modeled after the TV character played by Diahann Carroll—it was not until 1980 that Mattel introduced black dolls that were called Barbie. And as with what might be called their white subjective correlatives, these new dolls were made from the basic Barbie body mold and the same face mold that Mattel had used for a variety of dolls after 1972.[48] Cynthia Roberts writes:

At this point in America's social development, it's no longer necessary or desirable for an icon like Barbie to be identified exclusively as a Caucasian. So this year [1980], rather than expanding the ethnic base of Barbie's line by creating new "friends," Mattel simply comes out with black and Hispanic Barbies. It's an important moment in the doll's history. Now little girls of varied backgrounds can relate *directly* to Barbie.[49]

Mattel's promotional materials present the production of black, Hispanic, and Asian Barbie dolls as an attempt to give girls of all ethnicities (Mattel rarely if ever uses the word "race") subjects for self-identification and positive play. Ruth Handler insists that Barbie has achieved iconographical status precisely because "she allows girls from around the world to live out their dreams and fantasies in spite of a real world that may seem too big."[50] But Roberts, quite rightly, if inadvertently, relates these ethnic innovations to Mattel's awareness of the growing black and Hispanic middle classes, who have "more disposable income than ever before" and hence more money to spend on Barbie dolls and their accessories.[51] Though I don't mean to imply that there is no social conscience behind Mattel's policies, one doesn't have to be a cynic to think that profit is the major motive behind the peddling of multicultural wares.

In 1976, four years before Mattel entered the ethnic doll market in a big way, a press release for Shindana Toys—the same black-owned company Mattel helped to launch—made note of a growing demand for black dolls. Exulting over his product's success with white as well as black consumers, Shindana's president Robert Bobo predicted that "ethnically correct" dolls with real "Negroid features" were the wave of the future. Shindana's sales topped $1.4 million in 1975, according to Bobo, who went on to point out that other toy manufacturers and buyers had underestimated black spending power. The nation's 9.5 million black families "account for 10% of the U.S. toy and game purchases—amounting to some $350 million annually," the press release reported. The release ended with Bobo's observation that competition for black capital was heating up and that almost every major toymaker would soon be offering a line of black dolls.[52]

Shindana evidently felt that it had the edge over other toy manufacturers. But strutting its sales figures and predicting a boom in the popularity of ethnic dolls may have signed its death warrant. News that there was big money to be made from black dolls invited competition from companies far more solvent and better connected than Shindana. Despite the hope inscribed in its name, Shindana, which lacked the capital to promote its product aggressively, was poorly positioned to compete with the major toy manufacturers, which had more money to spend on advertising as well as long-term relationships with retail stores. In the early eighties Shindana began to flounder, just as Mattel began marketing black, Latina, and Asian Barbie dolls. As Mattel thrived, Shindana ceased production, closing its doors in June 1983.

Ironically, though its so-called ethnically correct "Negroid featured" dolls could not keep Shindana in business, the current Barbie boom may be one result of Mattel's own turn toward multiculturalism. In an effort to boost sales, Mattel announced in 1990 that it would go ethnic in its advertising by launching a campaign for black and Hispanic versions of the doll. Although some of these dolls had been around at least since the eighties, prior to the fall of 1990 Mattel's ads featured primarily white dolls. In what a *Newsweek* article describes as an attempt to capitalize on ethnic spending power, Mattel began placing ads for multicultural Barbie dolls in a variety of Afrocentric and Latin-oriented venues after its market research revealed that most black and Hispanic consumers were unaware of the company's ethnic dolls. This targeted advertising was a shrewd move because "Hispanics buy about $170 billion worth of goods each year, [and] blacks spend even more."[53] Indeed, sales of black Barbie dolls reportedly doubled in the year following this new ad campaign.

It is important to note, however, that Mattel introduced Shani—a black Barbie-like doll—in 1991, which may also have contributed to the rise in sales. This explanation seems likely since, to aid in the promotion of the Shani doll, Mattel engaged the services of a public relations firm that specializes in targeting black audiences. It is also worth noting that while Mattel may not have nationally advertised its black and Hispanic dolls until 1990, it had been selling those dolls in areas where there were large concentrations of blacks and Latinos since the early eighties.

Determined to present itself as politically correct as well as financially savvy, Mattel has been quick to point out that ethnic audiences, who are now able to purchase dolls who "look like them," are also profiting from the corporation's new marketing. Barbie is a role model for all of her owners, product manager Deborah Mitchell told *Newsweek*. "Barbie allows little girls to dream." Summarizing Mitchell's assertions, the *Newsweek* reporter concluded, seemingly without irony: "now, ethnic Barbie lovers will be able to dream in their own image."[54]

The notion of "dreaming in one's own image" is problematic of course, since dreams by definition engage something other than the real. But this is precisely the slippage Mattel encourages in marketing its ethnic dolls. The selling point is the promise of giving the other—the little black girl I was in the 1950s, for one—a self to play with who "looks like me." In other words, Mattel has entered the racist continuum I acknowledged the moment I realized that my dolls did not look like me.

Race and the Real Doll

"Realism is plausible," Catherine Belsey writes, "not because it reflects the world, but because it is constructed out of what is (discursively) familiar"[55]—what we already know or think we know, what we readily recognize and instantly decode. With its black, Hispanic, and Asian dolls and its Dolls of the World, Mattel attempts to reproduce a heterogeneous globe, in effect to produce multicultural meaning and market ethnic diversity. It does so, of course, not by replicating the individual differences of real bodies but by mass-marketing the discursively familiar—by reproducing stereotyped forms and visible signs of racial and ethnic difference.

But could any doll manufacturer or other image maker—advertising and film, say—attend to cultural, racial, and phenotypical differences without merely engaging the same simplistic big-lips/broad-hips stereotypes that make so many of us —blacks in particular—grit our (pearly white) teeth? What would it take to produce a line of dolls that would more fully reflect the wide variety of sizes, shapes, colors, hairstyles, occupations, abilities, and disabilities that African Americans—like all people—come in? In other words: what price difference? The cost of mass-producing dolls to represent the heterogeneity of the world would be far greater than either corporation or consumer would be willing to pay.[56] Mattel and other toymakers have gotten around this problem by making the other at once different and the same. In this sense, Mattel's play with mass-produced difference resembles the nation's uneasy play with a melting-pot pluralism that both produces and denies difference. That is to say, while professing colorblindness, the nation-state—faced with people rather than plastic—has never quite known what to do with the other, how to melt down those who "look different." From the Constitution's "three-fifths compromise" (1787) to California's Proposition 187 (1994), what to do with the other—the other's history, language and literature, and especially body—is a question that has upset the democratic applecart.[57]

The toy industry is only one of many venues where multiculturalism, posed as an answer to critical questions about inclusion, diversity, and equality, has collapsed into an additive campaign that augments but does not necessarily alter the Eurocentric status quo. Barbie "gone ethnic" by way of dye jobs and costume changes seems to me but a metaphor for the way multiculturalism has been used as a kind of quick fix by both liberal humanism and late capitalism. Made from essentially the same mold as what Mattel considers its signature doll—the traditional, blond, blue-eyed Barbie—tawny-tinted ethnic reproductions are both signs and symptoms of an easy pluralism that simply melts down and adds on a reconstituted other without transforming the established social order, without changing the mold.

So if today Barbie dolls do come in a rainbow coalition of colors, races, ethnicities, and nationalities, all of these dolls look remarkably like the stereotypical white Barbie, modified only by a dash of color and a change of clothes. That multiple races and ethnicities issue from the same mold should surprise no one. From Colored Francie of the 1960s to Soul Train Shani of the 1990s, Mattel has seized every opportunity to profit from shifts in racial, cultural, and social politics. It may also be worth noting that it isn't only matters of race and ethnicity from which Mattel has sought to profit by, shall we say, diversifying its assets. Nor is Colored Francie the only faux pas the sales campaigns have produced.

Ken, Barbie's perennial escort, has never been as popular as his precious gal pal, leading Mattel to speculate that it might be time for Barbie to get a new boyfriend. A survey done in the early 1990s showed that, while little girls wanted Barbie to stand by her man, they wanted that man to have a more contemporary look. So in 1993 Mattel introduced a hip version of the traditionally strait-laced Ken doll. Dubbed Earring Magic Ken, this nineties-kind-of-guy sports an earring in his left earlobe and a plastic version of two-toned, bleached-blond hair. Having left his three-piece suit behind in the closet as he came out, Earring Magic Ken is dressed in black hip-hugger jeans, a purple fishnet tank top, a simulated leather vest, and faux Italian loafers. Dangling from a cord around his neck is a large faux-metal band, which some consumers—much to Mattel's chagrin —quickly claimed as a "cock ring," a sign of Ken's hitherto closeted queer identity.

A fashion accessory with a practical application, cock rings, which among gay males seem to have a symbolic meaning similar to wedding bands, are worn around the base of the penis. According to one source, such a ring slipped on a flaccid penis traps blood in the organ during an erection, thus increasing sensitivity and prolonging orgasm.[58] In addition, cock rings are commonly worn dangling from a chain around the neck, as in the case of Earring Magic a.k.a. Gay Ken.

The alleged cock ring and what some read as the doll's other stereotypical queer accouterments—including the purple mesh tank top and the bleached, boy-toy hair—made this latest manifestation of Ken very popular, particularly among gay men and Barbie consumers with a keen eye for a collector's item. Mattel cried foul. It was not amused—or so it said—by these queer appropriations of its latest plaything. Ken is as straight as ever, the company protested; it's naughty-minded adults who are warped. But in the face of rising sales and virtual stampedes for "Queer Ken," Mattel initially seemed only moderately irritated with gay-sayers.

"It was not our intention to do anything other than to create a toy for kids," media-relations director Donna Gibbs told a reporter for the *Chicago Sun Times* in August 1993. Of the doll's adoption by members of the gay community, Gibbs reportedly said: "How lovely. Who would have thought it?"[59] But by the time I spoke with Gibbs a year later, Earring Magic Ken had been "retired," and Mattel was holding a much harder defensive line. The claim that Earring Magic Ken is gay is "outrageous," she told me. "It was purely innocent on Mattel's part." Though I didn't ask about the cock ring, Gibbs's own train of thought ran in that direction. Earring Magic Ken was part of a series of six Earring Magic Barbie dolls, all of which were designed for children to play with, she went on to explain. Ken, like the Barbie dolls in the series, came with a large ring and two charms, which could be suspended from the ring. The claim that this doll is gay, Gibbs concluded, is just another example of "adults putting their perceptions on something intended for children."[60]

It has been difficult for some queer theorists, cultural critics, and Barbie watchers to believe that no one at Mattel ever had any idea that Earring Magic Ken might be taken for gay. No multinational corporation could be that innocent across the boardroom, these skeptics argue. Some have gone so far as to suggest that Mattel was simply trying again to capitalize on the spending power of what has been dubbed the "newest minority." But, as with Colored Francie, the company misread the signs and was not prepared for the commotion that would arise over the bauble some consumers identified as sexual paraphernalia.

For Mattel the actual point of contention and source of outrage may be the extent to which the corporation found itself caught in its own contradiction. On the one hand, so-named Barbie Millicent Roberts and her boyfriend Ken Carson (always presented as "she" and "he" rather than "it")—both of Willow, Wisconsin, both of whom went to State College—are marketed as if they were real people in the real world. On the other hand, when their unrealistic body types come under fire, Mattel maintains that Barbie (notorious bosom and all) and Ken are merely innocent toys for tots and teens. Having long denied that there is any sexual subtext to their dolls, Mattel suddenly found itself in the position of having to assert Earring Magic Ken's heterosexuality: the ring around Ken's neck might as well have been a noose. An earring is one thing, but a cock ring is another. Bestseller or not, Earring Magic Ken had to go.[61]

As for Mattel's claims of absolute innocence and righteous outrage, while I am among those inclined to be suspicious of Mattel's motives, I also remember that this is the same corporation that came up with Colored Francie in the heyday of the black-power movement and with a talking doll that said "Math class is tough," despite decades of scathing criticism from feminists. Mattel has profited from any number of blunders or accidents. The most important questions are not really about the corporation's intent: the road to Wall Street has rarely been paved with good intentions. As with Mattel's other efforts to commodify alterity, the most intriguing questions are about what makes possible the mass production of difference. How does difference look? What signifies race? What are the signs of sexual orientation? The rise and fall of Earring Magic Ken becomes a much more interesting story if Mattel is in fact innocent—if in trying for "hip," the company came up with "gay." We have, then, another instance of capitalism's necessarily reductive reading of the very signs of difference it tries to exploit.

To Market, To Market

As the queenpin of a billion-dollar industry, Barbie reigns supreme at the intersection of gender and capitalism. Moreover, the tremendous boost in sales that accompanied Mattel's marketing of ethnic Barbie dolls may suggest a critical link between consumerism and multiculturalism. Though it seems clear that black consumers buy black Barbie dolls, it is also clear that others buy them too. Doll collecting is big business, and Mattel's ethnic dolls—particularly those in its Dolls of the World series—are designed and marketed at least as much with adult collectors in mind as with little girls. Donna Gibbs told me that the national dolls are intended more for adults, "although appropriate for children." She explained that Mattel cultivates a competitive market for these "premium value" dolls by producing them in limited quantities, issuing them strategically (two or three different nations or cultures each year), and retiring a given national doll after only a year or two on the market.[62]

Doll catalogues, buyers' guides, and classified ads in *Barbie Bazaar* suggest precisely how premium this value currently is. According to the *Collectors Encyclopedia of Barbie Dolls,* Colored Francie is now one of the most sought-after dolls ever produced by Mattel.[63] It may have been a flop when it appeared in 1967, but today, in mint condition, Colored Francie is worth between $700 and $900.[64] Finding this now premium-value vintage doll—especially finding it NRFB (never-removed-from-box)—is the dream of serious collectors. "With the quality of the ethnic dolls," writes Westenhauser, "Mattel has created a successful market of variety with Barbie that represents the racially diverse world in which we live." Saying perhaps more than she intends about difference as decoration, Westenhouser adds that "such a large variety of Barbie dolls turns any home into a museum."[65]

Questions about the ties between multiculturalism and capitalism are by all means larger than Barbie. But given the doll's status as an American icon, interrogating Barbie may facilitate an analysis of the commodity culture of which she is both part and product. What makes such an interrogation difficult, however, is the fact that Barbie simultaneously performs several disparate, often contradictory operations. On the one hand, ethnic Barbie dolls seem to color in the whitewashed spaces of my childhood. They give little colored girls toys to play with that look like them. On the other hand, this seeming act of racializing the dolls is accomplished by a contrapuntal action of erasure. In other words, Mattel is only able to racialize its dolls by blurring the sharp edges of the very difference that the corporation produces and profits from. It is able to make and market ethnicity by ignoring not only the body politics of the real people its dolls are meant to represent, but by ignoring the body politic as well—by eliding the material conditions of the masses it dolls up.

Here and elsewhere in commodity culture, this concurrent racing and erasing occurs precisely because big business both adores and abhors difference. It thrives on a heterogeneity that is cheaply reducible to its lowest common denominator—an assembly-line or off-the-rack difference that is actually sameness mass-reproduced in a variety of colors, flavors, fabrics, and other interchangeable options. For the most part, the corporate body is far less fond of more complex, less easily commodified distinctions—differences whose modes of production require constant retooling and fine-tuning. The exceptions here, of course, are the big-ticket specialty items—the handmade, one-of-a-kind originals and limited editions—which are intended not to be consumed rapidly by hordes who pay a little but to be acquired with deliberation by a few who pay a lot.

In today's toy world, race and ethnicity have fallen into the category of precious ready-to-ware difference. To be profitable, racial and cultural diversity—global heterogeneity—must be reducible to such common, reproducible denominators as color and costume. Race and racial differences—whatever that might mean in the grander social order—must be reducible to skin color or, more correctly, to the tint of the plastic poured into each Barbie mold. Each doll is marketed as representing something or someone in the real world, even as the political, social, and economic particulars of that world are not only erased but, in a curious way, made the same. Black Jamaican Barbie—outfitted as a peasant or a maid—stands alongside white English Barbie, who is dressed in the fancy riding habit of a lady of leisure. On the toystore shelf or in the collector's curio cabinet, maid and aristocrat enjoy an odd equality (they even sell for the same price), but this seeming sameness denies the historical relation they bear to each other as the colonized and the colonizer.

If we could line up the ninety or so different colors, cultures, and other incarnations in which Barbie currently exists, the physical facts of her unrelenting sameness (or at least similarity) would become immediately apparent. Even two dolls might do the trick: white Western Fun Barbie and black Western Fun Barbie, for example. Except for their dye jobs, the dolls are identical: the same body, size, shape, and apparel. Or perhaps I should say *nearly* identical because in some instances—with black and Asian dolls in particular—coloring and other subtle changes (slanted eyes in the Asian dolls, thicker lips in the black dolls) suggest differently coded facial features.

In other instances, when Barbie moves across cultural as opposed to racial lines, it is costume rather than color that distinguishes one ethnic group or nation from another. Nigeria and Jamaica, for instance, are represented by the same basic brown body and face mold, dolled up in different native garbs, or Mattel's interpretation thereof.[66] With other costume changes, this generic black body and face can be Marine Barbie or Army Barbie or even Presidential Candidate Barbie. Much the same is true of the generic Asian doll—sometimes called Kira—who reappears in a variety of different dress-defined ethnicities. In other words, where Barbie is concerned, clothes not only make the woman, they mark the racial and/or cultural difference.

Such difference is marked as well by the miniature cultural history and language lessons that accompany each doll in Mattel's international collection. The back of Jamaican Barbie's box tells us: "*How-you-du* (Hello) from the land of Jamaica, a tropical paradise known for its exotic fruit, sugar cane, breathtaking beaches, and reggae beat!" In an odd rendering of cause and effect, the box goes on to explain that "most Jamaicans have ancestors from Africa, so even though our official language is English, we speak patois, a kind of *Jamaica Talk*,' filled with English and African words.[67] For example, when I'm filled with *boonoonoonoos*, I'm filled with much happiness!" So written, Jamaica becomes an exotic tropical isle where happy, dark-skinned, English-speaking peasants don't really speak English.

Presented as if out of the mouths of native informants, the cultural captions on the boxes help to sell the impression that what we see isn't all we get with these dolls. The use of first-person narration lends a stamp of approval and a voice of authority to the object, confirming that the consumer has purchased not only a toy or a collector's item to display but access to another culture, inside knowledge of an exotic, foreign other. The invariably cheerful greetings and the warm, chatty tone affirm that all's well with the small world. As a marketing strategy, these captions contribute to the museum of culture effect, but as points of information, such reductive ethnographies only enhance the extent to which these would-be multicultural dolls make race and ethnicity collectors' items, contributing more to the stock exchange than to cultural exchange.

Shani and the Politics of Plastic

Not entirely immune to criticism of its identity politics, Mattel sought advice from black parents and specialists in early childhood development in the making and marketing of a new assortment of black Barbie dolls—the Shani line. Chief among the expert witnesses was the clinical psychologist Darlene Powell Hopson, who coauthored with her husband Derek Hopson a study of racism and child development, *Different and Wonderful: Raising Black Children in a Race-Conscious Society* (1990). As part of their research and clinical work, the Hopsons repeated a groundbreaking study conducted by the black psychologists Kenneth and Mamie Clark in the 1940s.

The Clarks used dolls to demonstrate the negative effects of racism and segregation on black children. When given a choice between a white doll and a black doll, nearly 70 percent of the black children in the study chose the white doll. The Clarks' findings became an important factor in *Brown v. Board of Education* in 1954. More recently, scholars have called into question both the Clarks' methodology and the meaning ascribed to their findings: the assumption that a black child's choosing a white doll necessarily reflects a negative self-concept.[68] William Cross has argued, for example, that the Clarks confounded two different issues: attitude toward race in general and attitude toward the self in particular. How one feels about race or what one knows of societal attitudes toward the racially marked is not always an index of one's own self-esteem; or, as Harriette Pipes McAdoo suggests, perhaps black children "are able to compartmentalize their view of themselves from their view of their racial group."[69]

Such qualifications—coupled with the evidence of my own experience (my dreaming through the white male persona of Glenn Evans as a child did not mean that I hated my black female self)—have also led me to question the Clark studies. For Darlene and Derek Hopson, however, the research remains compelling. In 1985 they repeated the Clarks' doll test and found that 65 percent of the black children in their sample chose a white doll over a black one. Moreover, 76 percent of the children interviewed said that the black dolls looked "bad" to them. Based on their own doll tests and their clinical work with children, the Hopsons concluded that black children, "in great numbers," continue to identify with white images—even when black images are made available. "Our empirical results confirmed the messages Black children were sending us every day in our practice," the Hopsons explain. "We're not as good, as pretty, or as nice as Whites . . . We don't like being Black. We wish we could be like *them*."[70]

The Hopson findings sent shock waves across the country and around the world. The interest their results generated among social scientists, parents, and the popular press prompted the Hopsons to write *Different and Wonderful,* a guidebook in which they use their experience as psychologists and as parents to suggest ways of counteracting negative racialized imagery. Several of their interventional strategies involve "doll play," and here again the ubiquitous Barbie has a featured role.

"If your daughter likes 'Barbie' dolls, by all means get her Barbie," the Hopsons advise black parents. "*But also* choose Black characters from the Barbie world."[71] Admittedly, I know more about word usage than about child psychology, but it seems to me that the Hopsons' own phrasing may speak to at least one problem with their positive play methodology and the role of Barbie in it. "Barbie," unmodified in the preceding statement, apparently means *white* Barbie, suggesting that the Hopsons also take white Barbie dolls as the norm. Black Barbie is toyland's "but also," just as black people are society's "but also."

The problem here is not simply semantic. Barbie has a clearly established persona and a thoroughly pervasive presence as a white living doll. The signature Barbies, the dolls featured on billboards, on boxes, in video and board games, on clothing, and in the Barbie exercise tape (as well as the actresses who play Barbie on Broadway and the models who make special appearances as Barbie at Disneyland and elsewhere) are always blond, blue-eyed, and white. Colorizing Barbie, selling her in blackface, does not necessarily make her over into a positive black image.

"My daughter wants to know why she can't have a white Barbie doll," one African American mother told me. "She's been playing happily with black Barbie dolls since she was two, but lately she wants to know why she can't have a white doll; why she can't have a *real Barbie.*" The four-year-old's words, like the Hopsons' "but also," speak to the larger color biases of imagery, texts, and toys that persist more than fifty years after the Clark study. If black children continue to identify with white images, it may be because even the would-be positive black images around them—including black Barbie dolls—serve to reinforce their second-class citizenship.[72]

But there may be other problems with the well-meaning advice offered black parents in *Different and Wonderful*. The Hopsons suggest that parents should not only provide their children with ethnic dolls but that they also should get involved in the doll play. "Help them dress and groom the dolls while you compliment them both," they advise, offering this routine: "This is a beautiful doll. It looks just like you. Look at her hair. It's just like yours. Did you know your nose is as pretty as your doll's?" They further recommend that parents use "complimentary words such as *lovely, pretty,* or *nice* so that [the] child will learn to associate them with his or her own image."[73]

Certainly it is important to help black children feel good about themselves, which includes helping them to be comfortable with their own bodies. One might argue, however, that these suggestions run the risk of transmitting to the black child a colorized version of the same old white beauty myth. Like Barbie dolls themselves, these techniques for positive play not only make beauty a desirable fixed physical fact—a matter of characteristics rather than character—they make this embodied beauty synonymous with self-worth. A better strategy might be to use the doll to show children how *unlike* any real woman Barbie is. In spite of their own good intentions, the Hopsons in effect have endorsed the same bill of goods Mattel has made the basis of its ethnically oriented marketing campaign—a campaign launched perhaps not entirely coincidentally in the fall of 1991, the year after the Hopsons' book *Different and Wonderful* appeared.

Though one can only speculate about a link between the publication of *Different and Wonderful* and Mattel's going ethnic in its advertising, it is clear that the Hopsons' strategies for using dolls to instill ethnic pride caught the company's attention.[74] In 1990 Darlene Hopson was asked to consult with Mattel's product manager Deborah Mitchell and designer Kitty Black Perkins—both African Americans—in the development of a new line of "realistically sculpted" black fashion dolls. Hopson agreed, and about a year later Shani and her friends Asha and Nichelle became the newest members of Barbie's entourage.

According to the doll's package:

> Shani means marvelous in the Swahili language . . . and marvelous she is! With her friends Asha and Nichelle, Shani brings to life the special style and beauty of the African American woman. Each one is beautiful in her own way, with her own lovely skin shade and unique facial features. Each has a different hair color and texture, perfect for braiding, twisting and creating fabulous hair styles! Their clothes, too, reflect the vivid colors and ethnic accents that showcase their exotic looks and fashion flair![75]

These words attempt to convey a message of black pride—after the fashion of the Hopsons' recommendations for positive play—but that message is clearly tied to bountiful hair, lavish and exotic clothes, and other external signs of beauty, wealth, and success.

Mattel gave Shani a coming-out party at the International Toy Fair in February 1991. Also making their debuts were Shani's friends Asha and Nichelle, notable for the different hues in which their black plastic skin comes—an innovation due in part to Darlene Hopson. Shani, the signature doll of the line, is what some would call brown-skinned; Asha is honey-colored; and Nichelle is deep mahogany. Their male friend Jamal, added in 1992, completes the collection.

The three-to-one ratio of the Shani quartet—three black females to one black male—may be the most realistic thing about these dolls. In the eyes of Mattel, however, Shani and her friends are the most authentic black dolls yet produced in the mainstream toy market. Billed as "Tomorrow's African American woman," Shani has broader hips, fuller lips, and a broader nose, according to Deborah Mitchell. Kitty Black Perkins, who has dressed black Barbies since their birth in 1980, adds that the Shani dolls are also distinguished by their unique, culturally specific clothes in "spice tones, [and] ethnic fabrics," rather than "fantasy colors like pink or lavender"[76]—evidently the colors of the faint of skin.

The notion that fuller lips, broader noses, wider hips, and higher derrieres make the Shani dolls more realistically African American again raises many difficult questions about difference, authenticity, and the problematic categories of the real and the symbolic, the typical and the stereotypical. Again we have to ask what authentic blackness looks like. Even if we knew, how could this ethnic or racial authenticity ever be achieved in a doll? Also, where capital is concerned, the profit motive must always intersect with all other incentives.

The Shani doll is an apt illustration of this point. On the one hand, Mattel was concerned enough about producing a more "ethnically correct" black doll to seek the advice of black image specialists in the development and marketing of the Shani line. On the other hand, the company was not willing to follow the advice of such experts where doing so would entail a retooling that would cost the corporation more than the price of additional dyes and fabrics.

For example, Darlene Hopson argued not just for gradations in skin tones in the Shani dolls but also for variations in body type and hair styles. But, while Mattel acknowledged both the legitimacy and the ubiquity of such arguments, the ever-present profit incentive militated against breaking the mold, even for the sake of the illusion of realism. "To be truly realistic, one [Shani doll] should have shorter hair," Deborah Mitchell has admitted. "But little girls of all races love hair play. We added more texture. But we can't change the fact that long, combable hair is still a key seller."

In fact, there have been a number of times when Mattel has changed the length and style of its dolls' hair. Christie, the black doll that replaced Colored Francie in 1968, had a short Afro, which was more in keeping with what was perhaps the signature black hairstyle of the sixties. Other shorter styles have appeared as the fashions of the moment dictated. In the early sixties, Barbie sported a bubble cut like Jacqueline Kennedy's.[77] Today, though, Mattel seems less willing to crop Barbie's hair in accord with fashion. Donna Gibbs told me that the long hair of Mattel's dolls is the result of research into play patterns. "Combing, cutting, and styling hair is basic to the play patterns of girls of all ethnicities," she said. All of the products are test-marketed first with both children and adults, and the designs are based on such research.[78]

Hair play is no doubt a favorite pastime with little girls. But Mattel, I would argue, doesn't simply respond to the desire among girls for dolls with long hair to comb; it helps to produce those desires. Most Barbie dolls come with a little comb or brush, and ads frequently show girls brushing, combing, and braiding their dolls' long hair. In recent years Mattel has taken its invitation to hair play to new extremes with its mass production of Totally Hair Barbie, Hollywood Hair Barbie, and Cut and Style Barbie—dolls whose Rapunzel-like hair lets down in seemingly endless locks. (Cut and Style Barbie comes with "functional sharp edge" scissors and an extra wad of attachable hair. Hair refill packs are sold separately.) But what does the transference of flowing fairy-princess hair onto black dolls mean for the black children for whom these dolls are supposed to inspire self-esteem?

In the process of my own archival research—poking around in the dusty aisles of Toys R Us—I encountered a black teenage girl in search of the latest black Barbie. During the impromptu interview that ensued, my subject confessed to me in graphic detail the many Barbie murders and mutilations she had committed over the years. "It's the hair," she said emphatically several times. "The hair, that hair; I want it. I want it!" Her words recalled my own torturous childhood struggles with the straightening combs, curling irons, and chemical relaxers that biweekly transformed my woolly "just like a sponge" kinks into what the white kids at school marveled at as my "Cleopatra [straight] hair."

Many African American women and quite a few African American men have similar tales about dealing with their hair or with the hair of daughters or sisters or mothers. In "Life with Daughters," the black essayist Gerald Early recounts the difficulties that arose when Linnet, the elder of his two daughters, decided that she wanted hair that would "blow in the wind," while at the same time neither she nor her mother wanted her to have her hair straightened. "I do not think Linnet wanted to change her hair to be beautiful," Early writes; "she wanted to be like everyone else. But perhaps this is simply wishful thinking here or playing with words, because Linnet must have felt her difference as being a kind of ugliness."[79]

Indeed, "colored hair," like dark skin, has been both culturally and commercially constructed as ugly, nappy, wild, and woolly, in constant need of taming, straightening, cropping, and cultivating.[80] In the face of such historically charged constructions, it is difficult for black children not to read their hair as different and that difference as ugly. Stories and pictures abound of little black girls putting towels on their heads and pretending that the towels are long hair that can blow in the wind or be tossed over the shoulder. But ambivalence about or antipathy toward the hair on our heads is hardly limited to the young. Adult African Americans spend millions each year on a variety of products that promise to straighten, relax, or otherwise make more manageable kinky black hair.[81] And who can forget the painful scene—made hilarious by Spike Lee and Denzel Washington in *Malcolm X*—in which his friend Shorty gives the young Malcolm Little his first conk?

Mattel may have a point. It may be that part of Shani's and black Barbie's attraction for little black girls—as for all children and perhaps even for adults—is the dolls' fairy-princess good looks, the crowning touch of glory of which is long, straight hair, combable locks that cascade down the dolls' backs. Even though it is not as easy to comb as Mattel maintains, for black girls the simulated hair on the heads of Shani and black Barbie may suggest more than simple hair play; it may represent a fanciful alternative to what society presents as their own less attractive, short, kinky, hurts-to-comb hair.

As difficult as this prospect is to consider, its ancillary implications are even more jarring. If Colored Francie failed in 1967 partly because of her "Caucasian features" and her long, straight hair, is Shani such a success in the 1990s because of those same features? Is the popularity of these thin-bodied, straight-haired dolls a sign that black is most beautiful when readable in traditional white terms? Have blacks, too, bought the dominant ideals of beauty inscribed in Barbie's svelte figure and flowing locks?

It would be difficult to answer these questions, I suppose, without making the kinds of reductive value judgments about the politics of black hair that Kobena Mercer has warned us against: the assumption that "hair styles which avoid artifice and look 'natural,' such as the Afro or Dreadlocks, are the more authentically black hair-styles and thus more ideologically 'right-on.'"[82] Suffice it to say that Barbie's svelte figure—like her long hair—became Shani's body type as well, even as Mattel claims to have done the impossible, even as they profess to have captured in this new doll the "unique facial features" and the "special style and beauty of the African American people." This claim seems to be based on subtle changes in the doll that apparently are meant to signify Shani's black difference. Chief among these changes—especially in Soul Train Shani, a scantily clad hiphop edition of the series released in 1993—is the *illusion* of broader hips and an elevated buttocks.

This illusion is achieved by a technological sleight of design that no doubt costs the company far less than all the talk about Shani's broader hips and higher derriere would suggest. No matter what Mattel spokespersons say, Shani—who has to be able to wear Barbie's clothes—is not larger or broader across the hips and behind than other Barbie dolls. In fact, according to the anthropologists Jacqueline Urla and Alan Swedlund, who have studied the anthropometry (body measurements) of Barbie, Shani's seemingly wider hips are if anything a fraction smaller in both circumference and breadth than those of other Barbie dolls. The effect of a higher buttocks is achieved by a change in the angle of the doll's back.[83]

On closer examination, one finds that not only is Shani's back arched, but her legs are also bent in and backward. When laid face down, other Barbie dolls lie flat, but the legs of Soul Train Shani rise slightly upward. This barely noticeable backward thrust of the legs also enhances the impression of protruding buttocks, the technical term for which is "steatopygia," defined as an excessive accumulation of fat on the buttocks. (The same technique was used in nineteenth-century art and photography in an attempt to make subjects look more primitive.) Shani's buttocks may appear to protrude, but actually the doll has no posterior deposits of plastic fat and is not dimensionally larger or broader than all the other eleven-and-a-half-inch fashion dolls sold by Mattel. One might say that reports of Shani's butt enhancement have been greatly exaggerated. Her signifying black difference is really just more (or less) of the same.

There is a far more important point to be made, however. Illusion or not, Shani's buttocks can pass for uniquely black only if we accept the stereotypical notion of what black looks like. Social scientists, historians, literary scholars, and cultural theorists have long argued that race is socially constructed rather than biologically determined. Yet, however coded, notions of race remain finely connected to the biological, the phenotypical, and the physiological in discussions about the racially marked body, not to mention the racially marketed body.

No matter how much scholars attempt to intellectualize it otherwise, "race" generally means "nonwhite," and "black" is still related to skin color, hair texture, facial features, body type, and other outward signifiers of difference. A less neutral term for such signifiers is, of course, stereotypes. In playing the game of difference with its ethnic dolls, Mattel either defies or deploys these stereotypes, depending on cost and convenience. "Black hair" might be easy enough to simulate (as in Kenyan Barbie's astro-turf Afro), but—if we buy what Mattel says about its market research—anything other than long straight hair could cost the company some of its young consumers. Mechanical manipulation of Shani's plastic body, on the other hand, represents a facile deployment of stereotype in the service of capital. A *trompe l'oeil* derriere and a dye job transform the already stereotypical white archetype into the black stereotype—into what one might call the Hottentot Venus of toyland.

Indeed, in identifying buttocks as the signifier of black female difference, Mattel may unwittingly be taking us back to the eugenics and scientific racism of earlier centuries. One of the most notorious manifestations of this racism was the use and abuse of so-called Hottentot women such as Sarah Bartmann, whom science and medicine identified as the essence of black female sexuality. Presented to European audiences as the "Hottentot Venus," Saartjie or Sarah Bartmann was a young African woman whose large buttocks (common among the people of southern Africa whom Dutch explorers called Hottentots or Bushmen) made her an object of sexual curiosity for white westerners traveling in Africa. According to Sander Gilman, for Victorians the protruding buttocks of these African women pointed to "the other, hidden sexual signs, both physical and temperamental, of the black female." "Female sexuality is linked to the image of the buttocks," Gilman writes, "and the quintessential buttocks are those of the Hottentot."[84]

Transformed from individual to icon, Bartmann was taken from Cape Town in the early 1900s and widely exhibited before paying audiences in Paris and London between 1910 and her death in 1915 at age twenty-five. According to some accounts, she was made to appear on stage in a manner that confirmed her as the primitive beast she and her people were believed to be. Bartmann's body, which had been such a curiosity during her life, was dissected after her death, her genitals removed, preserved under a bell jar, and placed on display at the Musée de l'Homme in Paris.[85] But as Anne Fausto-Sterling has argued so persuasively, even attempting to tell the known details of the exploitation of this woman, whose given African name is not known, only extends her victimization in the service of intellectual inquiry. The case of Sarah Bartmann, Fausto-Sterling points out, can tell us nothing about the woman herself; it can only give us insight into the minds and methodologies of the scientists who made her their subject.[86] Given this history, it is ironic that Shani's would-be protruding buttocks (even as a false bottom) should be identified as the site and signifier of black female alterity—of "butt also" difference, if I may be pardoned the pun. Georges Cuvier, one of several nineteenth-century scientists to dissect and to write about Bartmann, maintained that the black female "looks different"; her physiognomy, her skin color, and her genitalia mark her as "inherently different."[87] Long since recognized as morbidly racist, the language of Cuvier's "diagnosis" nevertheless resembles the terms in which racial difference is still written today. The problems that underpin Mattel's deep play with Shani's buttocks, then, are the very problems that reside within the grammar of difference in contemporary critical and cultural theory.

From Bell Jar to Bell Curve

With Shani and its other black Barbie dolls, Mattel has made blackness simultaneously visible and invisible, at once different and the same. What Mattel has done with Barbie is not at all unlike what society has done with the facts and fictions of difference over the course of several centuries. In theoretical terms, what's at stake in studying Barbie is much more than just fun and games. In fact, in its play with racial and ethnic alterity, Mattel may well have given us a prism through which to see in living color the degree to which difference is an impossible space—antimatter located not only beyond the grasp of low culture but also beyond the reach of high theory.

Just as Barbie reigns ubiquitously white, blond, and blue-eyed over a rainbow coalition of colored optical illusions, human social relations remain in hierarchical bondage, one to the other, the dominant to the different. Difference is always relational and value-laden. We are not just *different;* we are always *different from.* All theories of difference—from Saussure and Derrida to Fanon and Foucault—are bound by this problematic of relativity. More significantly, all notions of human diversity necessarily constitute difference as oppositional. From the prurient nineteenth-century racism that placed Sarah Bartmann's genitals under a bell jar, to the contemporary IQ-based social Darwinism that places blacks at the bottom of a bell curve, difference is always stacked up against a (superior) center. This is the irony of deconstruction and its failure: things fall apart, but the center holds remarkably firm. It holds precisely because the very act of theorizing difference affirms that there is a center, a standard, or—as in the case of Barbie—a mold.

Yet, however deep its fissures, deconstruction—rather than destruction—may be the closest we can come to a solution to the problem for which Barbie is but one name. Barbie, like racism (if not race), is indestructible. Not even Anna Quindlen's silver-lamé stake through the doll's plastic heart would rid us of this immovable object, which is destined to outlive even its most tenacious critics. (This is literally true, since Barbie dolls are not biodegradable. Remembering the revenge the faithful took on Nietzsche—"'God is dead,' signed Nietzsche" / "'Nietzsche is dead,' signed God"—I can see my obituary in *Barbie Bazaar:* "'duCille is dead,' signed Barbie.") But if, as Wordsworth wrote, we murder to dissect, deconstructing Barbie may be our only release from the doll's impenetrable plastic jaws, just as deconstructing race and gender may be the only way out of the deep space or muddy waters of difference.

The particulars of black Barbie illustrate the difficulties and dangers of treating race and gender differences as biological stigmata that can be fixed in plastic and mass-reproduced. But if difference is indeed an impossible space—a kind of black hole, if you will—it is antimatter that continues to matter tremendously, especially for those whose bodies bear its visible markings and carry its material consequences.

The answer, then, to the problematic of difference cannot be, as some have argued, that gender does not exist or that race is an empty category. Such arguments throw the body out with the murky bath water. But, as black Barbie and Shani also demonstrate, the body will not be so easily disposed of. If we pull the plug on gender, if we drain race of any meaning, we are still left with the material facts and fictions of the body—with the different ifs, ands, and butts of different bodies. It is easy enough to theorize difference in the abstract, to posit "the body" in one discourse or another. But in the face of real bodies, ease quickly expands into complexity. To put the question in disquietingly personal terms: from the ivory towers of the academy I can criticize the racist fictions inscribed in Shani's false bottom from now until retirement, but shopping for jeans in Filene's Basement, how am I to escape the physical fact of my own steatopygic hips? Do the facts of my own body leave me hoisted not on my own petard, perhaps, but on my own haunches?

We need to theorize race and gender not as meaning*less* but as meaning*ful*—as sites of difference, filled with constructed meanings that are in need of constant decoding and interrogation. Such analysis may not finally free us of the ubiquitous body-biology bind or release us from the quagmire of racism and sexism, but it may be at once the most and the least we can do to reclaim difference from the molds of mass production and the casts of dominant culture.

Yet, if the process of deconstruction also constructs, tearing Barbie down runs the risk of building Barbie up—of reifying difference in much the same way that commodity culture does. Rather than representing a critical kiss of death, readings that treat Barbie as a real threat to womankind—a harbinger of eating and shopping disorders—actually breathe life into the doll's plastic form. This is not to say that Barbie can simply be reduced to a piece of plastic. It is to say that hazard lies less in buying Barbie than in buying into Barbie, internalizing the larger mythologies of gender and race that make possible both the "like me" of Barbie and its critique. So, if this is a cautionary tale, the final watchword for consumers and critics alike must be not only *caveat emptor* but also *caveat lector:* let the buyer and the reader beware.

2

Monster, She Wrote: Race and the Problem of Reading Gender-Wise

"Love, Oh love, Oh careless love." That's the story. It's in the songs. It's in the books. And everybody knows it . . . The only problem is that the story almost everybody knows is almost totally false.

—Lerone Bennett, "The Roots of Black Love" (1981)

Writing in *Ebony* in August 1981, the black historian Lerone Bennett accused black writers of creating "a new literature based on the premise that Black America is a vast emotionless wasteland of hustlin' men and maimed women." As Bennett heard and read them, lines and lyrics about ceaseless sex and heedless love, like those immortalized by Bessie Smith in "Careless Love," have helped to construct a false history of tortured gender relations among African Americans. Such lyrics, like a great deal of modern black literature, in Bennett's view, tell the false story of a "Black love deficit." "As a matter of hard historical fact," he writes, "the true story of Black love—love colored by, love *blackened* by the Black experience—is the exact opposite of the traditional myth." The "true story" is that "Black men and women—despite slavery, despite segregation, *despite every-*

thing—created a modern love song in life and art that is the loveliest thing dreamed or sung this side of the seas."[1]

Bennett's true story—what Deborah McDowell might call his black family romance[2]—is seductive. It affirms what many African American men and women would like to believe about our past and the possibilities for our future *together*. But the story of an all-enduring black love is indeed a plot many modern-day African American writers have rejected in favor of what some have labeled literary gender baiting and male bashing.

Bennett named no one in particular in his indictment of artists who got the story wrong, but scores of other black male scholars and critics have pointed accusing fingers at such writers as Alice Walker, Toni Morrison, Gayl Jones, Ntozake Shange, and Gloria Naylor. These women are chief among the many black female artists charged not only with historical inaccuracy but with racial infidelity—putting their gender before their race, their (white) feminism before their black family—and inventing historical fictions that serve a feminist rather than an Afrocentric or black nationalist agenda.

Indeed, for black women, membership (real or assumed)[3] in the sisterhood of feminists is in some circles an unpardonable sin punishable by excommunication, if not from the race, certainly from the ranks of those who have authored the sacred texts of the race. As one pair of critics put it: black feminists have drawn "a simplistic sex line in society" that has put them "on the wrong side of some fundamental questions."[4] One can be black *or* a woman, but claiming both identities places one on shaky familial ground, outside the romance.

In the minds or, more important, in the critiques of influential black men of letters such as Addison Gayle and Ishmael Reed, contemporary black women authors have not only miswritten the romance, but they have slandered black men in the process. As McDowell notes in her incisive reading of this dubious battle of the sexes, where "female readers see an implicit affirmation of *black women*," many male readers see "a programmatic assault on black men."[5] What is for female writers like

Walker a commitment "to exploring the oppressions, the insanities, the loyalties, and the triumphs of black women" is for male readers like Gayle and Reed "a hatchet job" directed viciously against black men or a libel campaign akin to "the kind of propaganda spread by the Ku Klux Klan and the American Nazi party."[6] What is for black women an effort to write themselves into history is for Gayle and Reed a malicious form of mythmaking that holds black men hostage to a portrait of the past too painful to be anything but a lie. Addison Gayle has spoken in a telling way to this nagging question of historical truth: "If we look at [Alice Walker's] work in history," he said in an interview, "particularly if there is any great deal of accuracy in her portrayal of Black men, then we're in more trouble than I thought we were, *and I thought we were okay.*"[7]

In this chapter I argue that in the consumption and production of literature, masculinism masquerading as neutral, we're-okay critique should be called by its rightful name, just as racism needs to be acknowledged in the real world. Many of the black male critics I call upon use race and racial fidelity in much the same way that the right uses Americanism and patriotism; that is to say, black nationalism denies sexism in much the same way that white nationalism denies racism. It is not just a matter of my country or my race right or wrong, but of denying the wrongs in order to proclaim the right. Just as Newt Gingrich reads past Thomas Jefferson's racism in order to proclaim him an exemplary American, certain black male critics—for the sake of the race—want black women to write past the sexism of black men.

I have no wish merely to resurrect ancient arguments that pit black men against black women or to retrace ground ably covered by others.[8] Nor do I mean to imply that male readers have been singularly disdainful of the "feminist fictions" of contemporary black women writers or that only male readers have offered such criticism.[9] Instead I want to explore from a slightly different angle some of the vexing gender-loaded assumptions and resonant racial imperatives that underpin many male critiques of black women's fiction: (1) that there is an essential black experience; (2) that there is an absolute historical truth; (3) that art absolutely must tell the truth; (4) that black men and women in America are "okay" in their erotic relations with one another. I want to examine what's at stake in a race-conscious, gender-bound criticism in which "black is beautiful" is the only truth—the sole story (or maybe soul story)—we are allowed to tell.

Because art is invention, "truth" has long since been exposed as a false standard by which to evaluate an artist's work. This should be the case whether the issue is Alice Walker's representation of black men or Spike Lee's treatment of black women. Yet this is precisely the leap of faith that many critics of African American literature continue to make. Texts are transparent documents that must tell the truth as *they* know it. Failure to tell *their* truth not only invalidates the text; it also discredits, deauthorizes, and on occasion deracializes the writer. But truth, like beauty, is in the eye and the experience of the beholder.

The beholder metaphor invites us to question the authority of the critical *I* to invent the other it beholds, even in the midst of reading the other's celebration of self. As black men and women, our racial alterity makes us perpetually other, perpetually beheld. But what happens when blacks read each other, when the beheld becomes the beholder, when black men read black women reading black men? How does a black male reader position himself as the center of seeing in a female-authored text? Must the beheld always be seen in terms of her difference from the beholder? Is it possible for the male *I* to read a female text without reinscribing hierarchies of one kind or another, without in effect defacing the woman beheld?

Although I generally shy away from efforts to define distinctly male and female ways of knowing, here I want to take the risk of gender essentialism and codify this great divide as a battle between subjectivities, between male and female stories, between phallocentric and gynocentric "truths." This collision of genders is all the more difficult to tease out, it seems, because of the collusion of race—the shared racial alterity—that historically has made it hard to be at once black and a woman.

My own readings of history and literature are necessarily colored by my indivisible blackwomanness, but my purpose is not to attack male critics, masculinism, phallocentrism, or what Elaine Showalter calls "phallic criticism." I come in effect to praise Caesar, not to bury him—to legitimize phallic criticism, not to condemn it. Phallocentrism and masculinism are pejoratives that make men jumpy in the same way that accusations of racism make white people defensive. My own use of the terms, however, is practical, based on the belief that as scholars or critics or intellectuals we need to be up front about the roles that sex and gender play in shaping our interpretive strategies. We need to engender the critical *I* and call masculinist as well as feminist criticisms by their rightful names.

An important step in this naming ceremony is to surrender the myth that our shared racial alterity—our common American experience of slavery, institutionalized racism, and discrimination—makes black men and women brothers under the skin, okay with each other. "The enemy is not Black men," Addison Gayle has said, and "not Black women, it's this country."[10] I can hardly quarrel with the point that both black men and black women have been victims of American racism, but Gayle's "we're okay" rendition of African American history carries with it a decidedly masculine bias that factors out sexism.

Reading, Writing, and Romance

If we did not know it before, we have only to look as far as the Thomas-Hill hearings to see that black men and women in America are no more okay than the patriarchal system that reared us. That system historically has exacted not only submission from women but silence about whatever abuses it has chosen to inflict. Such silence was demanded of Anita Hill, as it continues to be demanded of black women writers. In speaking and writing sexism as well as racism, black women like Hill, Walker, Morrison, and Jones have committed what male criticism reads as racial heresy. They have broken with what I call the "discourse of deference"—a nationalistic, masculinist ideology of uplift that demands female deference in the cause of empowering the race by elevating its men.

This is precisely the charge that Mel Watkins levels against Jones, Shange, and Walker in his infamous review in the *New York Times:*

> those black women writers who have chosen black men as the target have set themselves outside of a tradition as old as black American literature itself. They have, in effect, put themselves at odds with what seems to be an unspoken but almost universally accepted covenant among black writers.[11]

In other words, by naming as oppressors black men as well as white, black women novelists are acting outside black history, writing outside the racial fold, the colored community. But Watkins's community is first and foremost the world of men. Since he acknowledges in the same article that until recently the most acclaimed black fiction writers were men, the ancient tradition to which he refers is not a "universally accepted covenant" but an understanding among men—a kind of gentlemen's agreement that suborns female silence in the name of racial empowerment.

In a far more generous though still male-identified reading of African American women's literature, W. Lawrence Hogue attributes this break with history to the influence of the feminist discourse of the sixties. Drawing on Michel Foucault's concept of discursive formation,[12] Hogue argues that Walker's first novel *The Third Life of Grange Copeland* (1970)—along with other feminist texts such as Jones's *Corregidora* (1975) and *Eva's Man* (1976) and Morrison's *The Bluest Eye* (1970) and *Sula* (1973)—invents its own African American historical myths in order to validate its feminist assumptions about women's reality. He praises the novel for its attempt to show how the pressures of white patriarchy cause black men "bruised and beaten by the system" to abuse their wives and children, even as he argues that the novel manipulates certain historical facts to meet its feminist agenda.[13]

Hogue, I think, makes an important theoretical move in acknowledging feminist fiction as invention. In practice, though, he seems ultimately (and, I suspect, inadvertently) to evaluate this invention in terms of its relation to male truths, male experience, and male narratives. Novels like *The Third Life*, he argues, are silent about the thousands of black men who refused to be dehumanized by the system—men who "maintained their humanity, their integrity, and their sanity by turning honestly and genuinely to the church and Christianity" —men who "vehemently defied the system, even at the expense of their own lives."[14]

As examples of heroic black men, Hogue offers Ernest Gaines's characters Ned Douglass and Jimmy Aaron from *The Autobiography of Miss Jane Pittman* (1971) and Marcus Payne from *Of Love and Dust* (1967). Like Aaron and Douglass, Payne "refuses to accept the constrictions of the system. He strikes out against it and meets his death." Although he also attends to the silences in black male-authored texts elsewhere in his book, Hogue's invocation of Gaines's heroes sets up a comparative analysis in which Walker's novel is found wanting yet again for its failure to celebrate black manhood. Moreover, in the discursive formation of his own argument, Hogue transforms important textual "facts" and remains silent about certain significant details. He does not mention, for example, that Marcus Payne strikes out against the system in somewhat the same fashion as Alice Walker's character, Brownfield Copeland—with his penis—by sleeping with the white boss's white wife. Seemingly following the advice of Eldridge Cleaver, Gaines has created in Marcus Payne a character who screws the white man by screwing his wife, a character who in effect uses his own tool to dismantle the master's house and is destroyed in the process.

Though part of a book that admirably attempts equal-opportunity criticism, Hogue's analysis of *The Third Life* and other feminist texts depends on his reading of certain male-authored and -authorized novels. While he acknowledges that books such as *Miss Jane Pittman* and *Of Love and Dust* are informed by black nationalism of the 1960s (as Walker's work is informed by sixties feminism), he does not fully address how these strategies are also gendered. He fails to note, for example, that the same black nationalist ideology, "which emphasizes the courage and dignity of Afro-Americans both past and present," is also tied to an understanding of the past so inherently masculine—so subliminally rooted in the phallus—that sleeping with the white overseer's wife is presented as a revolutionary act. Put another way, in this decidedly male-centered reading of African American literature and history, penile erection is equated with political insurrection.

Critical Differences

The difference between Gaines's sense of history and heroism and Walker's is a critical difference—which may cut to the heart of the controversy over male and female texts, maculinist and feminist readings. It may be that at the heart of this controversy lie not only different notions of truth, art, and history, but very different readings of the phallus and the penis. What Houston Baker reads as the cosmic force of the black phallus in *Invisible Man* (1952), for example, Toni Morrison writes as the black penis that rapes and impregnates a twelve-year-old girl in *The Bluest Eye* (1970). What for Ralph Ellison is symbolic action is for Morrison a father raping his daughter. What for Baker is an aristocratic procreativity turned inward is in Morrison's novel "a bolt of desire [that] ran down [Cholly Breedlove's] genitals, giving it length." What Baker calls "outgoing phallic energy," Morrison names inbreeding lust, bordered by politeness that makes a father want to fuck his daughter—tenderly. "But the tenderness would not hold," Morrison writes in parodic undertones, which at least one male critic has mistaken for sympathy.[15] "The tightness of her vagina was more than he could bear. His soul seemed to slip down to his guts and fly out into her, and the gigantic thrust he made into her then provoked the only sound she made—a hollow suck of air in the back of her throat."[16]

It is interesting to note that Baker repeatedly uses the term *phallus*—as Lacanian signifier, the originator of meaning—when he talks about the action of the penis. As he himself observes elsewhere: "The PHALLUS is, of course, to be distinguished from the penis. The PHALLUS is not a material object but a signifier of the Father, or, better, of the Father's LAW."[17] Morrison's portrait of incest complicates what both Ellison and Baker have oversimplified. It reminds us that signifier and signified are not so easily separable. For though the phallus may not be a material object, its action, its "phallic energy," is not immaterial—certainly not to Matty Lou Trueblood, Pecola Breedlove, and other objects of its power.

Baker's reading, like Ellison's narrative, erases the penis that rapes the daughter as it privileges the phallus that fathers what Baker describes as the entire tribe of Afro-America. His interpretation is, in perhaps the most literal sense possible, phallic criticism. But again my motive in labeling it such is to denature it, to wrest it of the illusion of universality and to confirm that it, like feminist criticism, is situational, vested with a variety of imperatives and perspectives.

The effort to denature masculinist criticism must make an important second move, however—one that resists polarizing the interpretive process along easily drawn gender lines. It is not only men who do such readings and such readings are not the only kind male critics do. For example, one of the sharpest analyses of the gender biases of both Ellison's novel and Baker's reading has come from a black male scholar, Michael Awkward. Calling *The Bluest Eye* a "purposefully feminist revision" of Ellison's masculinist reading of incest, Awkward writes: "Baker's essay mirrors the strategies by which Trueblood (and Trueblood's creator) validates male perceptions of incest while, at the same time, silencing the female voice or relegating it to the evaluative periphery."[18]

The Peter Principle

In prose, poetry, and song, modern black women attempt to speak through such silences. Complementing and by all means challenging male perspectives with their own, they offer up different and often difficult somebody-done-somebody-wrong songs that not only indict black men as well as white but that also identify the love of men as the root of women's oppression. Zora Neale Hurston's character Nanny makes such an identification in *Their Eyes Were Watching God* (1937). "Dat's de very prong all us black women gits hung on," she tells her granddaughter Janie. "Dis love! Dat's just whut's got us uh pullin' and uh haulin' and sweatin' and doin' from can't see in de mornin' till can't see at night."[19] In placing these words in her character's mouth—identifying "dis love" as a devastating force in the lives of black women—Hurston gave voice to a concern that reverberates throughout modern African American women's fiction. From Jessie Fauset and Nella Larsen writing in the 1920s to Walker and Morrison writing in the 1990s, black women novelists have been consistently concerned with exploring on paper what Hortense Spillers calls "the politics of intimacy"[20] and with confronting the consequences, burdens, and mixed blessings of love, men, and marriage.

But Hurston is also signifying, I think. For the prong on which women are impaled is not simply "dis love" but "dat penis," the domain of dominance. One of my male colleagues has accused me of overreading in making this claim. "'Dis love,'" he insists, "is just love." But I remain convinced that this sexual double-entendre, like so many others in *Their Eyes,* is Hurston's invention, not mine. Part of what catches women up, Hurston seems to say, is not just their penchant for confusing sex and love, love and marriage, dream and truth, but their tendency to measure manliness by the same yardstick as men, to believe like men in the power vested in the penis.

Janie's implicit understanding of penile power is made explicit when she calls Joe out, as it were—when she finally responds in kind (and then some) to his harassment. After years of verbal and physical abuse, Janie delivers a fatal blow to her husband's power source by telling him publicly that all he is is a big voice. To Joe's taunt that she "ain't no young gal no mo'" she replies:

> Naw, Ah ain't no young gal no mo' but den Ah ain't no old woman neither. Ah reckon Ah looks mah age too. But Ah'm uh woman every inch of me, and Ah know it. Dat's uh whole lot more'n *you* kin say. You big-bellies around here and puts out a lot of brag, but 'tain't nothin' to it but your big voice . . . When you pull down yo' britches, you look lak de change uh life.[21]

So saying, Janie announces that the mighty Mayor Joe Starks is sexually inadequate, he can't get it up, he's not enough man for "every inch" of woman she still is. It is significant, of course, that Janie reckons her sexuality by the male measurement of inches. Hers is a series of well-placed punches that land below the belt, that not only rob Joe of "his illusion of irresistible maleness" but that metaphorically *feminize* him by linking his impotence to female menopause, "de change uh life." In the wake of these words, Joe's "vanity bled like a flood." It is a bloodletting—a symbolic castration—that ends in the mayor's death.

Like Janie, Mem Copeland—Brownfield's brutalized wife in *The Third Life*—eventually shifts the balance of power in her marriage by attacking her husband with a shotgun strategically aimed at his genitals. Thrusting the "cool hard gun barrel down between his thighs," Mem for a moment acts outside the submissive role she has accepted for nine years. "To think," she tells Brownfield at gunpoint, "I put myself to the trouble of wanting to git married to you . . . And just think how many times I done got my head beat by you just so you could feel a little bit like a man."[22] Wielding the shotgun (described as smooth and black and big) and threatening to shoot off her husband's balls if he doesn't abide by her rules, Mem negotiates a better life for herself and the family. She moves them out of their rat-infested country shack into a city house, "a 'mansion' of four sheet-rocked rooms." The jobs she finds for herself and for Brownfield bring a sense of progress and newfound, if short-lived, prosperity to the Copeland household.

"If he had done any of it himself," the text tells us, "if he had insisted on the move, he might not have resisted the comfort" that Mem's ingenuity bestows on the family. Instead Brownfield's bruised manhood flares tragically, and he plots to destroy his wife by using her own body against her, twice impregnating her in a calculated attempt to undermine her already fragile health. Mem's shotgun was a great equalizer, but ultimately Brownfield's penis proves the more powerful weapon: "You thought I fucked you 'cause I wanted it," he says to Mem in bitter triumph. "Your trouble is you just never learned how not to git pregnant." Some radical feminists might argue that in surrendering to heterosexual desire Mem is collaborating with her own assassin. For, not content with nearly impregnating her to death, Brownfield eventually shoots and kills Mem. Patriarchy in this text is indeed black as well as white, and its penile oppression is lethal.

Toni Morrison gives a similarly oppressive, though less physically violent, face to patriarchy in *Song of Solomon* (1977). She too locates the source of man's abusive power between his legs. "You have never picked up anything heavier than your own feet or solved a problem harder than fourth-grade arithmetic," her character Magdelene called Lena says to her brother Milkman. "Where do you get the *right* to decide our lives? I'll tell you where. From that hog's gut that hangs down between your legs." As a parting shot at her brother and the value system and gender codes that have made his male life of greater value than her female life, Lena says: "You are a sad, pitiful, stupid, selfish, hateful man. I hope your little hog's gut stands you in good stead, and that you take good care of it, because you don't have anything else."[23] Lena's message to Milkman resembles Janie's message to Joe. Although this verbal assault on male genitalia does not kill or castrate, it does send Milkman Dead on a search that takes him into a different quality of life and manhood.

The Love Jones

If dominative male power is indeed located below the belt, disempowering men means not simply placing the penis under scrutiny but under erasure. This is precisely the action the title character takes in Gayl Jones's controversial second novel *Eva's Man*. After a month as "the willing prisoner of Davis Carter's love"[24]—to use one critic's contradictory characterization—Eva Medina Canada first poisons the man who has held her captive and then mutilates his dead body by severing his penis with her teeth.

> I opened his trousers and played with his penis. My mouth, my teeth, my tongue went inside his trousers. I raised blood . . . I got back on the bed and squeezed his dick in my teeth. I bit down hard . . .
> I got the silk handkerchief he used to wipe me after we made love, and wrapped his penis in it. I laid it back inside his trousers, zipped him up.[25]

Davis becomes for Eva an Everyman, and so he is made to atone for the sins of a myriad of men (and an eight-year-old boy with a dirty popsicle stick) who have sexually abused her throughout her life. But here too it is not simply men who are under attack but the penis.

Coming on the heels of *Corregidora* the year before, the publication of *Eva's Man* in 1976 set off a hue and cry among many black male critics, for whom Davis Carter's mutilated member is evidently more than phallus, more than simply signifier.

While the specter of a bloody, gnawed, dismembered member is surely horrifying for all audiences, it is no doubt particularly so for male readers whose connection to the severed organ is more than metaphorical. Yet there is more at issue in the negative critical reception of *Eva's Man* than castration anxiety, just as there is more at stake in the controversy over feminist texts than their negative portrayals of black men. Black men do not necessarily fare well in such sacred, male-authored texts as *Native Son, Go Tell It on the Mountain,* and *Invisible Man.* Yet these novels continue to be championed by the same critics who condemn *Eva's Man.* Moreover, the castration of the protagonist in *Invisible Man* is accepted as symbolic in a way that Davis Carter's castration is not, even though for all its graphic language it too, I would argue, is metaphoric. What is actually at stake are the larger questions: Who holds the power? Who owns the black body? Who can tell the black story? Who can write the true black history? Who gets to say "I'm okay"? Who gets to sing the authentically blues? All of these questions are played out *masterfully* in Gayl Jones's first novel.

Corregidora is literally and figuratively a blues novel; more specifically, in its treatment of erotic coupling and marriage, *Corregidora* is "dearly beloved blues"—my name for a particular variety of art that focuses (often as a lament) on the problems of married life and romantic relations.[26] On the literal level, this is the story of a blues singer, Ursula "Ursa" Corregidora, the last in a long line of black women haunted by history—by a legacy of rape, incest, and patriarchal psychosexual abuse, passed down through four generations like a family heirloom. The novel recounts Ursa's brief marriage in 1947 to Mutt Thomas—their breakup after only four months, after trying to work through Mutt's inability to accept Ursa's need to sing—and the couple's reunion twenty-two years later. In a figurative sense, the blues are the extended metaphor around which Jones works the magic of her text, the medium she uses to enable Ursa to tell her story.

Ursa is the great-granddaughter of an evil Portuguese slave-master named Corregidora, who prostituted and impregnated the women he owned, including his own daughter, Ursa's grandmother. Despite the unspeakable nature of Corregidora's crimes and the destruction of all records of those crimes, the task with which Ursa—like her mother, grandmother, and great-grandmother before her—has been entrusted is to *speak* Corregidora's evil: to "make generations" that will bear witness to his cruelty and abuses.

After a drunken Mutt causes Ursa to fall down a flight of stairs, she loses the child she is carrying and is forced to have a hysterectomy, leaving her physically unable to make generations. This is only part of her problem, however, only part of the difficulty Ursa has in loving Mutt or Tadpole (the cafe owner she marries briefly) or Cat or Jeffy (women friends who represent the possibility of lesbian love). Corregidora's larger problem lies in the contradiction and dishonesty of Great Gram's charge to her to make generations. Making generations, as Janice Harris has pointed out, means making love; but making love for the purpose of making evidence turns what should be a positive act into an act of vengeance: "The goal of lovemaking subverts the act; the end denies the means."[27]

What Ursula must face is not only the crippling contradiction inherent in Great Gram's charge but the emotional ambivalence beneath it: a tangle of mixed emotions and conflicting loyalties that were no doubt present in a great many sexual liaisons between master and slave, owner and property. The question Ursa must confront in her own life is the one that only her father, Martin, has the courage to ask of her grandmothers: "How much was hate for Corregidora and how much was love?"

When at the end of the novel, a forty-seven-year-old Ursula is reunited with Mutt after a separation of two decades, she asks herself the same question. "You never would suck it," Mutt says as Ursa takes his penis into her mouth. "You never would suck it when I wanted you to. Oh, baby . . . I didn't think you would do this for me."[28] At the moment when she holds Mutt delicately suspended between pleasure and pain, Ursa understands what it was that her great-grandmother did to the man who owned her, making him hate her one minute and unable to get her out of his mind the next. "It had to be sexual . . . it had to be something sexual that Great Gram did to Corregidora." In this moment of understanding—in "a split second of hate and love"—Ursa realizes her power as well: "I could kill you," she says (though it is unclear whether this is thought or spoken, for we are told immediately, "He came and I swallowed"). Love and hate are so intertwined that even or perhaps especially at the moment of giving intense sexual pleasure, *she could kill him.*

Unlike the tormented heroine of *Eva's Man,* Ursa does not kill Mutt. Instead, she swallows Mutt's semen in a sexual act that will not make generations, an act that can be read metaphorically as swallowing the past—not forgetting it, as Mutt would wish, but taking it inside as an act of reconciliation rather than carrying it outside as a weapon of revenge. The act of fellatio, then, suggests a loosening of the bonds that have kept Ursa yoked to Corregidora; it signals Ursa's acceptance of the past, as Jones herself has said, as "an aspect of her own character, identity and present history."[29]

Melvin Dixon suggests that the climax of the novel is still an act of vengeance. "Ursa avenges herself on Mutt," he argues, "by performing fellatio on him—an act that places her in control." The mouth of the blues singer becomes, in Dixon's words, "an instrument of direct sexual power."[30] This is a possible reading, one that a number of critics have endorsed and one that the text invites. In such a reading, performing fellatio empowers the female because of her ability to disempower—dismember—her partner with one bite. I wonder if this empowerment isn't illusory, though; if the penis isn't, in this instance, indeed dematerialized as phallus. A sleeping John Wayne Bobbit notwithstanding, just how long would a wide-awake specimen lie passive as his penis is being bitten off?

Jones elides this question in *Corregidora* by making the assault a fantasy, a theory, and in *Eva's Man* by having Eva poison Davis before she dismembers him. Most critics have elided the question altogether. One exception is Richard Barksdale, who is so intent on making his case for female mandibular empowerment (Mother JAW as a counterpoint to Father LAW) that he even rewrites the novel so that "during an act of fellatio [Eva] mutilates her lover *and leaves him to bleed to death.*"[31]

In any case, if *Corregidora*'s poetic closure can be read as an act of revenge and empowerment, perhaps it also can be read as suggesting female surrender. Ursa's mouth doesn't become a powerful instrument through the act of fellatio; it has always been a powerful instrument. In singing the blues—singing her mother's songs and her own—she has used her mouth as her mother and grandmothers used their wombs. She has, in effect, made generations in song; her survival has depended on her voice; she has sung "because it was something [she] had to do."[32] With her "hard voice," a voice so hard it "hurts you and makes you still want to listen," Ursa has both participated in and perpetuated an oral tradition. Her final act of oral reconciliation may also be an act of self-silencing—where Ursa's hard voice is not simply softened but literally silenced by Mutt's penis. Will Ursa still sing the blues in the morning and, if so, whose blues will they be?

And what about the ideology of empowerment at work here? It troubles me that so many critical discussions about *Corregidora* define reconciliation and what Dixon calls "successful coupling" in terms of who has power over whom sexually. Moreover, the role that so many critics (especially men) see as empowering the female—the privilege of performing fellatio on the man who for most of the novel has been more patriarch than partner—seems to me to confirm Ursa in precisely the role Mutt has wanted for her all along: as "his woman," the instrument of his pleasure. The novel's ending can be read as a reconciliation certainly, but it also can be read as male sexual gratification: Ursa finally does for him what she would not do before. Mutt acknowledges as much himself: "I didn't think *you would do this for me.*"

The question of power and pleasure becomes even more complex if we consider it in terms of both *Corregidora* and *Eva's Man*. Eva achieves the climax with Elvira Moody, her woman cellmate, that Ursa does not achieve with Mutt. Yet it is Ursa and Mutt's sexual reunion that many critics read as the successful coupling. Mutt's pleasure is expressed: "Oh, baby." "He came and I swallowed." Ursa's is assumed. Yet it is this encounter that Melvin Dixon describes as the more active lovemaking—a positive counterpoint to "the unrelenting violence, emotional silence, and passive disharmony in *Eva's Man*."[33]

"Tell me when it feels sweet," Elivra says to Eva in the final moments of *Eva's Man*. "Tell me when it feels sweet, honey." "I leaned back, squeezing her face between my legs," Eva says, "and told her, 'Now'" (p. 177). Eva, as Dixon reads her, allows herself to be seduced by Elvira, "passively receiv[ing] her in the act of cunnilingus," unlike Ursa, who, through the act of fellatio, "brings Mutt within the orbit of her physical control." I would argue that the language of the encounter is hardly passive. Eva squeezes Elvira's face between her legs and *speaks* her own pleasure—"Now"—in a way she has not done before. Dixon's otherwise sensitive reading ultimately privileges the male principle, implying that it is better for a woman to give pleasure to a man than to take it with another woman. Throughout the novel, Eva has been "trapped in the prison of her own emotions," but will she remain there, trapped in "her choice of silence," "forever singing solo," as Dixon suggests? *"Now"*: I'm not so sure.

The novel ends in an ambiguity. Elvira Moody may be just another in a long line of men and women who abuse Eva, who take advantage of her. Or, as Ann Allen Shockley suggests, she may do no more in the novel than provide "a background litany of on-going seduction."[34]—a seduction to which Eva finally submits simply because there is no man around, because she can't keep knocking Elvira out of bed. But when read in light of the fellatio in *Corregidora*, the cunnilingus that brings Eva (and *Eva's Man*) to climax may suggest something else entirely. It may suggest a way off the prong "dat all us black women gits hung on": not necessarily lesbian sexuality, but definitely paying less attention to male gratification and more to our own. In other words: making ourselves the subjects of our own stories, our own lives.

Perhaps this is what has been difficult for many black male readers to accept: seeing themselves depicted as something other than the heroes of *their* women's lives, seeing the black penis portrayed as something other than the royally paternal phallus. They have misread the refusal of a certain kind of male behavior as a rejection of black men. Such a misreading seems to underpin Addison Gayle's criticism not of Gayl Jones's work but of her. Protesting that black women novelists only write about black men as "white folks' Toms" or "brutes à la *Corregidora*," Gayle suggests that "if Gayl Jones believes that Black men are what she says they are, she ought to get a white man."[35] So saying, Gayle shifts the venue of literary criticism from the written fictions of the text to the assumed facts of the author's life, while at the same time questioning the writer's allegiance to the race she supposedly betrayed with her pen.

In such appraisals the beholder exceeds his authority as reader. He extrapolates a universal real—"all black men"— from the particular fiction—"a black man" or "some black men." At the same time, he denigrates the woman writer by assigning to her the attitudes, problems, proclivities, and conflicts of her characters, denying her the courtesy of creative imagination.

In general, black women writers have weathered the storms of criticism. But Gayl Jones, by her own admission, has been made "extremely 'double conscious'" by criticisms that assume that "the fictional invention must imply something about the personal relationships or the way I think 'black men are.'"[36] Although she has not been completely silenced, the kind of vitriolic, overly personalized censure her first two novels received in some circles has changed the course of her writing, particularly her attention to sexuality. "I had to force myself to go ahead with such scenes in *The Stone Dragon*," she says, "because they belonged there, but they're not as graphic and they don't use the same kind of vocabulary (that was true of the characters) of *Eva's Man* and *Corregidora*." Though she, like Walker, remains committed to exploring relationships between men and women, in most of her later work Jones either changes the race and gender of her antagonists or avoids sexual scenes altogether.

That any writer would feel called upon to change the race, gender, or actions of her characters because some readers are unable, as Jones says, to "see beyond those details of erotic consciousness to other meanings" is a travesty of both the creative and the critical process. It makes literary criticism an act of violence that ironically reinscribes the same oppressive, patriarchal attitudes refracted in the literature.

Ishmael Reed, articulating the sentiments of many black male readers, has asked black women writers why they feel the need to castrate the black man.[37] One answer may be: because, like the mountain, sexism is there. The novel and other literary forms have given black women a forum for exploring the oppression, insanities, sorrows, joys, and triumphs of women's lives and for transforming those experiences into art.

Clifford Geertz suggests that all art forms render ordinary experience comprehensible.[38] Using Geertz's theory to explain the persistence of rape fantasies in white women's romantic fiction, Janice Radway argues that "the romance's preoccupation with male brutality is an attempt to understand the meaning of an event that has become almost unavoidable in the real world."[39] Writing rape into the romance, Radway suggests, is a way for women to work through the misogynistic attitudes that run so deeply in our society. A similar claim can be made for both the preoccupation with the politics of sexuality and the attention to male violence and penile oppression in the novels of writers such as Morrison, Walker, and Jones. Their fictions are not about doing a hatchet job on black men as mates but about claiming women as the authors of their own lives, rather than as objects of desire in a truth-as-*I*-know-it history of blacks in America that is actually the truths of men.

Like a number of black male critics, Darryl Pinckney resists the effort to supplement male truths with female perceptions. He protests that in *The Color Purple* "the black men are seen at a distance . . . entirely from the point of view of women."[40] Well, yes. From whose point of view is Miss Jane Pittman seen or Bessie in *Native Son* or Matty Lou Trueblood in *Invisible Man?* It is surely impossible to have a literature or a criticism utterly without gender perspective, without male or female perceptions. In the realm of African American literary studies, both the texts and the interpretations of black men have been treated as if they were indeed without such perspective—without male perceptions. They have been treated simply as *the truth.*

Readings are never neutral. All criticisms are local, situational. My own interpretations are colored by my race and my gender, by my blackness and my feminism. I readily label what I do "black feminist criticism." Masculinist criticism needs to be similarly willing to label itself and its biases. But what the field needs is not only more truth in advertising, as it were, but more introspection. For all of us—masculinists, feminists, womanists—the challenge of critical practice is to see both inside and outside our own assumptions. Texts have a way of becoming what we say they are. But what's at stake is not merely the fidelity we owe to the books we read but the way we do our jobs, our own intellectual integrity. Many black male scholars have accused contemporary black women writers of wielding words like a sword. It remains to be seen whether the woman writer's sword is mightier than the pen is.

3

The Occult of True Black Womanhood

Truth is, I never thought I'd see the day when people would be interested in hearing what two old Negro women have to say. Life still surprises me. So maybe the last laugh's on *me*.

—Annie Elizabeth ("Bessie") Delany, *Having Our Say*

Today there is so much interest in black women that I have begun to think of myself as a kind of sacred text. Not me personally, of course, but me as black woman, the other. Within the modern academy, racial and gender alterity has become a hot commodity that has claimed black women as its principal signifier. I am alternately pleased and perturbed by this, by the alterity that is perpetually thrust upon African American women, by the production of black women as infinitely deconstructable "othered" matter. Why are black women always other? To myself, I am not other; to me it is the white women and men so intent on theorizing my difference who are the other. Why are they so interested in us? Why have black women become the subjected subjects of so much contemporary scholarly investigation, the peasants under glass of intellectual inquiry in the 1990s?

The attention is not altogether unpleasant, especially after generations of neglect, but I am hardly alone in suspecting that the interest in black women may have as much to do with the pluralism and even the primitivism of this particular postmodern moment as with the genuine quality of black women's accomplishments and the breadth of their contributions to American civilization. It is not news that, by virtue of our race and gender, black women are not only the second sex—the other, in postmodern parlance—but also the last race, the most oppressed, the most marginalized, the most deviant, the quintessential site of difference. And through the inversions of deconstruction, feminism, cultural studies, multiculturalism, and the contemporary commodity culture, the last shall be first, perhaps.

I say *perhaps* because we have experienced such inversions before: such as the preoccupation, in the 1920s, with black women, the blues, black folk, the authentic, the real colored thing, a preoccupation fueled by the primitivist bent of that historical moment. In the twenties, the fascination with the black female body in particular, and the primitive sexual appetite attributed to the African woman, increased the degree to which the black woman functioned as an erotic icon in the racial and sexual ideology of western civilization.

The black feminist theorist bell hooks calls the contemporary version of this preoccupation with difference "the commodification of Otherness," or "eating the Other." "Within commodity culture," she writes in *Black Looks*, "ethnicity becomes spice, seasoning that can liven up the dull dish that is mainstream white culture." Mass culture, then, perpetuates the primitivist notion "that there is pleasure to be found in the acknowledgment and enjoyment of racial difference."[1]

Where gender and racial difference meet in the bodies of black women, the result is the invention of an other Otherness, a hyperstatic alterity. Mass culture, as hooks argues, produces and perpetuates the commodification of otherness through the exploitation of the black female body. In the 1990s, however, the main sites of exploitation are not simply the cabaret, the speakeasy, the music video, the glamor magazine; they are also the toy industry, the academy, the publishing business, the intellectual community. In the words of Houston Baker, "Afro-American women's expressivity and the analyses that it has promoted during the past two decades represent the most dramatically charged field for the convergence of matters of race, class, and gender today."[2] Of course, one of the dangers of standing at an intersection—particularly at such a suddenly busy, three-way intersection—is the likelihood of being run over by oncoming traffic.

Michele Wallace likens the particular traffic jam that has built up around Zora Neale Hurston to a rainbow coalition of critics who, "like groupies descending on Elvis Presley's estate," are engaged in "a mostly ill-mannered stampede to have some memento of the black woman" who is, at least to some degree, a figment of their individual and collective critical imaginations.[3]

I want to explore what it means for black women academics to stand in the midst of the "dramatically charged field"—the traffic jam—that black feminist studies has become. Are we in the way of the critical stampede that accompanies what I am calling "the occult of true black womanhood"? Are we in danger of being trampled by the rainbow coalition of critics—"black, white, male, female, artists and academics, historicists and deconstructionists"—that our own once isolated and isolating intellectual labors have attracted to the magnetic field of black feminist studies?

Hurstonism and Black Feminism

In her foreword to the 1978 reprint of *Their Eyes Were Watching God,* Sherley Anne Williams tells of first encountering Zora Neale Hurston and *Their Eyes* as a graduate student enrolled in a two-semester survey of black poetry and prose. "Afro-American literature was still an exotic subject then," Williams writes, "rarely taught on any regular basis."[4] She goes on to describe how she and her classmates fought over the pitifully few copies of African American texts, long out of print, that they were able to beg or borrow from musty basements, rare-book collections, and reserved reading rooms. When it finally became her turn to read *Their Eyes,* Williams says she found in the speech of Hurston's characters her own country self and, like Alice Walker and many others, became Zora Neale's for life.

For those of us who came of intellectual age in the late sixties and early seventies, Williams's discovery of Zora Neale is an almost painfully familiar textual encounter of the first kind. Though Hurston was not the first black woman writer I encountered or claimed as my own (that was Ann Petry), it was during this same period, 1971, that I too discovered Zora. I was introduced to her work by my friend and fellow graduate student, Gayl Jones. When I began my teaching career a few years later at Hamilton College in New York, Gayl was again generous enough to lend me her well-worn copy of *Their Eyes.* Only a lingering fear of being prosecuted for copyright infringement prevents me from detailing how I went about sharing among the dozen or so students in my seminar, none of whom had heard of Hurston, the fruits that bloomed within the precious, tattered copy of *Their Eyes Were Watching God.*

Twenty-five years later, African American literature courses and black women writers are again exotic subjects. They are exotic this time out, however, not because they are rarely taught or seldom read, but because in the midst of this multicultural moment, they have become politically correct, intellectually popular, and commercially precious. Once altogether ignored as historical and literary subjects or badly misfigured as magnanimous mammies, man-eating matriarchs, or immoral Jezebels, black women—that is, certain black women—and their texts have been taken up by the academy, invoked by the intellectual elite as well as the scholarly marginal. Currently in print in several editions, *Their Eyes Were Watching God* has become quasi-canonical, holding a place of honor on reading lists in mainstream history courses, in social science, literature, and American studies, as well as in those more marginalized disciplines, African American studies and women's studies. Much the same holds true for Walker's *The Color Purple* and Morrison's *Beloved,* each of which has been awarded a Pulitzer Prize for fiction (with Morrison's oeuvre winning her the Nobel Prize for literature in 1993 as well).

It is important to note that black women critics and scholars have played a crucial role in bringing to the academic fore the works of "lost" writers such as Hurston and Nella Larsen and in opening up spaces within the academy both for the fiction of contemporary African American women writers and for the study of women of color more generally. Though I am usually suspicious of efforts to define benchmarks and signposts, there are a number of important essays, anthologies, and monographs that can be rightly claimed as the founding texts of contemporary black feminist studies. Toni Cade's anthology *The Black Woman* (1970), for example—which showcased the prose and poetry of writers such as Nikki Giovanni, Audre Lorde, Paule Marshall, Alice Walker, and Sherley Anne Williams—stands as a pivotal text along with critical essays and literary, historical, and sociological studies by Barbara Smith, Barbara Christian, Frances Beal, Joyce Ladner, Jeanne Noble, Darlene Clark Hine, Angela Davis, Frances Foster, Filomina Chioma Steady, Sharon Harley and Rosalyn Terborg-Penn, and Mary Helen Washington.[5]

While keepers of culture have given the lion's share of credit for the development of black literary and cultural studies to male scholars such as Houston Baker, Henry Louis Gates, and Cornel West, Mary Helen Washington has been a key player in efforts to define and institutionalize the fields of African American literature and black feminist studies for more than twenty years.[6] Among my most precious possessions is a tattered copy of the August 1974 issue of *Black World,* which contains an article by Washington called "Their Fiction Becomes Our Reality: Black Women Image Makers." In this article, one of the first pieces of black feminist criticism I discovered (and in others that began appearing in *Black World* in 1972), Washington reviewed the work of black women writers such as Gwendolyn

Brooks, Maya Angelou, Ann Petry, and Toni Cade Bambara, as well as Walker, Marshall, and Morrison.

Much the same can and must be said of Barbara Christian and Barbara Smith, whose essays on African American women writers began appearing in print in the mid and latter 1970s. Christian's first book, *Black Women Novelists: The Development of a Tradition, 1892–1976* (1980), which brilliantly analyzed the work of black women writers from Frances Harper to Walker, remains a foundational text: "the Bible in the field of black feminist criticism," according to Michele Wallace.[7] Nor have nearly twenty years dulled the impact and significance of Barbara Smith's "Toward a Black Feminist Criticism" (1977), a widely reprinted, often anthologized black lesbian feminist declaration that gave name, definition, and political persuasion to the perspective from which Bambara, Washington, and others had been writing.[8] Smith's work in literary criticism and that of her sister Beverly Smith in the area of black women's health have played crucial roles in developing the fields of black feminist and black lesbian studies.

Within the realm of literary studies alone, the names on even a partial list of pioneering black feminist scholars are, as Houston Baker has said, legion: Deborah McDowell, Nellie McKay, Hortense Spillers, Gloria Hull, Patricia Bell Scott, Cheryl Wall, Valerie Smith, Mae Henderson, Gloria Wade-Gayles, Thadious Davis, Trudier Harris, Frances Smith Foster, Hazel Carby, Joyce Joyce, and Claudia Tate, as well as Christian, Washington, Smith, and many others.[9] Both as an inspiration to aspiring writers and as an editor at Random House in the 1970s, Toni Morrison has played a particularly dramatic role in opening up spaces for critical attention to African American women.

As a beneficiary of their research and writing, I am anxious to give credit where it is long overdue, but this chapter is not intended as a praisesong for black women scholars, critics, and artists or as a review of the literature they have generated.[10] Instead I would like to examine some of the consequences of the current explosion of interest in black women as literary and historical subjects. Among the issues I explore are the ways in which this interest—which seems to me to have reached occult status—increasingly marginalizes both the black women critics and scholars who excavated the fields in question and their black feminist "daughters" who would further develop those fields.

What does it mean, for instance, that many prestigious university presses and influential literary publications regularly rely not on these seasoned black women scholars but on male intellectuals—black and white—to review the manuscripts and books of young black women just entering the profession? What does it mean for the black female professoriate that departments ask powerful senior black male scholars to referee the tenure and promotion cases of the same black women scholars who have challenged these men in some way? What does it mean for the field in general and for junior African Americanists in particular that senior scholars, who are not trained in African American studies and whose career-building work often has excluded black women, are now teaching courses in and publishing texts about African American literature and generating "new scholarship" on black women writers? What does it mean for the future of black feminist studies that a large portion of the growing body of scholarship on black women is now being written by white feminists and by men whose work frequently achieves greater critical and commercial success than that of the black female scholars who carved out the field?

My questions are by no means new; nor do I claim to have any particularly insightful answers. I only know that as one who has been studying the literature and history of black women for almost thirty years and teaching it for more than twenty, I have a burning need to work out my own ambivalence and, at times, animosity over the newfound enthusiasm for these fields that I think of as my own hard-won territory. It is a little like the parent who tells the child she is about to reprimand that "this hurts me more than it hurts you." But lest anyone think this an easily authored Portnoy's complaint in blackface—yet another black womanist indictment of white feminists who can do no right and men who can do only wrong—I want to make explicit my own uneasy antagonism.

Elsewhere I have argued against territoriality, against essentialism, against treating African American studies as the private property of what Gayatri Spivak calls "black blacks."[11] Yet questions of turf and appropriation persist, despite my best efforts to intellectualize them away. Here again my dilemma is neither new nor mine alone. The modern version of the ageless argument over who owns the sacred text is at least as old as the work of the white anthropologists Melville and Frances Herskovits, dating back to the 1920s and reaching a controversial peak in 1941 with the publication of *Myth of the Negro Past,* a study of African cultural retentions scorned by many black intellectuals. It was in the fifties, however, that white scholars began to loom large in black historiography and literary criticism, often receiving within the academy a kind of attention that the pioneering work of many black historians and critics had not enjoyed. The black historian Darlene Clark Hine noted in 1980 that "most of the highly-acclaimed historical works were, with few exceptions, written by white scholars." In fact, the legitimization of black history as a field proved a "bonanza for the [white] professional historians already in positions [as university professors and/or recognized scholars] to capitalize from the movement."[12]

Some 130 years ago, Harriet Jacobs was able to publish her life story only with the authenticating stamp of the well-known white abolitionist Lydia Maria Child. "I have signed and sealed the contract with Thayer & Eldridge, in my name, and told them to take out the copyright in my name," Child wrote in a letter to Jacobs in 1860. "Under the circumstances *your* name could not be used, you know."[13] The circumstances were of course the conditions of slavery under which Jacobs had lived for most of her life and from which she had not completely escaped. Now, as then, it often seems to take the interest of white scholars to legitimize African American history and literature or such "minority discourses" as postcoloniality and multiculturalism. Let me offer two examples: Gerda Lerner's *Black Women in White America* (1972) and Shelley Fisher Fishkin's *Was Huck Black?* (1993).

The black feminist Gloria Wade-Gayles has identified Toni Cade [Bambara]'s *The Black Woman* (1970) as "the first book that pulled together black women's views on black womanhood" and Jeanne Noble's *Beautiful, Also, Are the Souls of My Black Sisters* (1978) as the "first history of black women in America written by a black woman."[14] Yet, despite the recovery and reconnaissance missions of Bambara, Noble, Joyce Ladner, and other black women intellectuals who did groundbreaking work in the seventies, it is the white feminist Gerda Lerner whom the academy recognizes as the pioneer in reconstructing the history of African American women.

With the 1972 publication of her documentary anthology *Black Women in White America,* Lerner became by many reckonings the first historian to produce a book-length study devoted to African American women. Her goal was to call attention to such "unused sources" as black women's own records of their experiences and "to bring another forgotten aspect of the black past to life." In drawing on such first-person accounts as diaries, narratives, testimonies, organizational records and reports, Lerner endeavored in her volume, she says, "to let black women speak for themselves."[15]

The notion of letting someone speak for herself is troubling, but we might note too that Lerner was by no means the first to draw on so-called unexamined resources. Black artists, activists, and intellectuals have been making use of these resources at least since the nineteenth century. The former slave William Wells Brown, for one, drew on such sources in the many novels, narratives, and histories he published between 1847 and his death in 1884. The black activist, educator, and "race woman" Anna Julia Cooper spoke for herself and on behalf of multitudes when she wrote of the "long dull pain" of the "open-eyed but hitherto voiceless Black Women of America" in *A Voice from the South,* published in 1892.[16] Although written in a vein quite different from Lerner's, Mrs. N. F. Mossell's *The Work of the Afro-American Woman*, first published in 1894, represents an early effort on the part of an African American woman to acknowledge the accomplishments of her black sisters. Hallie Q. Brown's *Homespun Heroines and Other Women of Distinction* (1926), which offered minibiographies of a host of black women from Phillis Wheatley to Madame C. J. Walker, is another. Their own joys, sorrows, and the testimonies of other African American women, poor women, working women, were the imperatives that propelled much of the political activism among black clubwomen at the turn of the century.

Nor should we ignore the intellectual labors of the black literary scholar Charles Nichols, whose masterwork, *Many Thousand Gone: The Ex-Slaves' Account of Their Bondage and Freedom* (1963), has directed two generations of researchers interested in slavery to a significant source: the "forgotten testimony of its victims." Although Nichols merits only a brief mention in the bibliographical note at the end of *Black Women in White America,* the methodology that Lerner employs in her book is one he perfected.[17]

To take up a more contemporary example, I can point out that for decades black writers, critics, and scholars have been delineating the impact that African American culture has had on the mainstream literary tradition. Their efforts have received little attention from the academy. But when a white scholar recently asked if Huckleberry Finn were black, the academy, the publishing industry, and the media sat up and took notice. I am referring, of course, to the hoopla over Shelley Fisher Fishkin's *Was Huck Black?* (1993). As much as a year before it appeared in bookstores, Fishkin's study was lauded in the *New York Times, Newsweek,* and the *Chronicle of Higher Education.* In fact, according to the London *Times,* more than fifty news items on the book appeared across the country, with such headlines as: "Scholar Concludes that Young Black Was Model for Huck Finn's Voice"; "Huck Finn Speaks 'Black,' Scholar

Says"; and "Theory Might Warm Foes to Twain's Novel."[18] I quote from one article that appeared in the *Chronicle:*

> Ms. Fishkin's book, *Was Huck Black? Mark Twain and African-American Voices,* is likely to have a major impact, not just on the way scholars interpret a mainstay of the American literary canon, but also on the way scholars define that canon. By calling attention to the way multicultural voices have influenced mainstream literature, it suggests that traditional views of the dichotomy between majority and minority cultures may be flawed. In so doing, the book gives the term multiculturalism a new meaning.[19]

Fishkin's work is unquestionably important and provocative. What intrigues me, however, is the response from the white intellectual establishment. Why is the conclusion that "we need to pay more attention to African-American culture, even when we study the canon" suddenly being greeted as news? Black scholars have long argued the reflexive nature of cultural appropriation and the interrelatedness of so-called minor and major traditions. Speaking at a socialist conference in 1917, James Weldon Johnson, whom David Levering Lewis calls the "dean of Afro-American letters," shocked his audience by declaring that "the only things artistic in America that have sprung from American soil, permeated American life, and been universally acknowledged as distinctly American were the creations of Afro-Americans."[20] It should come as no surprise to scholars that Mark Twain, like many major white American writers, took canon fodder from "the black experiences" that are a fundamental part of American culture.

These examples suggest a kind of color line and an intellectual passing within and around the academy: black culture is more easily intellectualized (and canonized) when transferred from the danger of lived black experience to the safety of white metaphor, when you can have that "signifying black difference" without the difference of significant blackness. Fishkin's work, like Lerner's, is undeniably significant, but it does not stand alone. "Sociable Jimmy," the black boy on whose vernacular speech Mark Twain may have based Huck's colorful language, never got to speak for himself in print, but black women had been speaking for themselves long before Gerda Lerner endeavored to let them do so.

As I have suggested, the question of who speaks for me, who can write my sacred text, is as emotionally and politically charged as it is persistent and controversial. Asked about the explosion of interest in the lives and literature of black women among male scholars and white feminists, Barbara Christian responded:

> It is galling to me that after black women critics of the 1970s plowed the neglected field of Afro-American women's literature when such an act was academically dangerous, that some male and white feminist scholars now seem to be reaping the harvest and are major commentators on this literature in influential, though not necessarily feminist journals such as *The New York Review of Books*. Historical amnesia seems to be as much a feature of intellectual life as other aspects of American society.[21]

Historical amnesia may displace her at any time, but for now at least, the black woman writer is a bonanza. Her popularity as subject matter has spawned a wealth of critical scholarship and has led scores of scholars to claim her material and cultural production as their intellectual discourse. But as Barbara Christian implies, black women's expressivity is not merely discourse; it has become lucre in the intellectual marketplace, cultural commerce. What for many began as a search for our mothers' gardens, to appropriate Alice Walker's metaphor, has become for some a Random House harvest worth millions in book sales and university professorships.

Sensitive as the issue is, it must be said at some point, and even at the risk of hurt feelings, that the explosion of interest in the black female subject is in some measure about economics, about jobs. The white scholar Elizabeth Abel has acknowledged as much. "This new attentiveness [to texts by women of color] has been overdetermined," she argues, "by the sheer brilliance and power of this writing and its escalating status in the literary marketplace and, consequently, the academy; [and] by white feminist restlessness with an already well-mined female literary tradition."[22] For many scholars trained in these well-mined fields, the shift to African American studies has yielded more prominent positions at more prestigious institutions.

But is this necessarily a bitter harvest? African American women scholars have complained long and loud about exclusion, about the degree to which white feminists and male critics have ignored the work of black women. Can we now legitimately complain that they are taking it up? And what do such complaints tell us about ourselves and our relationship to what many of us continue to speak of as *our* literature?[23]

While I too am troubled by what at times feels like the appropriation of black women by white feminists and by men, what I want to get at here is not simply about property rights. It is not my intention to claim Hurston, Morrison, or Walker as the private property of black women readers who see themselves in the fictional characters. Rather than liberating and valorizing black female voices, in fact, the celebration of African American women's literature and history as the discursively familiar, as a "truth" to which black women scholars have privileged access, both limits and demeans those discourses. However inadvertently, it restricts this work to a narrow orbit in which it can be validated only by those black women for whom it reproduces what they already know.[24]

Undeniably, contributions to the study of black women and their literature and history have been made by scholars who are neither black nor female. William L. Andrews comes to mind immediately, as does Robert Hemenway. That we have increased access to the autobiographical writings of nineteenth-century African American women is due in part to Andrews's effort. That Hurston's work is now being read is due in no small measure not only to Alice Walker but also to Hemenway. Through the efforts of the white scholar Jean Fagan Yellin and the black theorist Henry Louis Gates, to cite two other examples, we now have access to two fundamental texts from the nineteenth century: Harriet Jacobs's *Incidents in the Life of a Slave Girl, Written by Herself* (1861) and Harriet Wilson's *Our Nig* (1859). Moreover, since 1988 the Schomburg Library of Nineteenth-Century Black Women Writers, of which Gates is general editor, has made available dozens of previously lost texts. The recent work of the white scholar Elizabeth Ammons also represents a positive turn in literary studies. In its intercultural readings, her book *Conflicting Stories: American Women Writers at the Turn into the Twentieth Century* (1992) is a model of its kind.

Surely this is good news. Why then am I and so many other black feminist scholars left with the obdurate questions about cooptation and exploitation? Why are we haunted by a growing sense that we are witnessing (and perhaps even inspired) the commodification of the same black womanhood we have championed? It is a mistake, I think, to define this persistent debate over who can read black female texts as strictly or primarily racial or cultural or gendered: black/white, male/female, insider/outsider, our literature/your theory, my familiar/their foreign. The most important questions may not be about essentialism and territoriality, biology, sociology, or even ideology but, rather, about professionalism; about cultural literacy and intellectual competence; about taking ourselves seriously and insisting that we be taken seriously not simply as objects in someone else's histories—as native informants—but as artists, scholars, and critics reading and writing our own literature and history.

When Demeanor Demeans

So I have arrived at what for me is the heart of the matter. Much of the newfound interest in African American women that seems to honor the field of black feminist studies actually demeans it by treating it not like a discipline with a history and a body of rigorous scholarship underpinning it, but like an anybody-can-play pickup game played on an open field. Often the object of the game seems to be to reinvent the intellectual wheel: to boldly go where in fact others have gone before, to flood the field with supposedly new "new scholarship" that evinces little sense of the discipline's genealogy. Moreover, many of the rules that the academy generally invokes in doing its institutional business—making appointments, assigning courses, promoting faculty—are suspended when what is at stake is not the valorized, traditional disciplines of western civilization but the more marginal, if popular, fields within African American studies.

Among those elements considered when English departments hire medievalists, Victorianists, Americanists, and such, are schools attended, the nature of your graduate training, the subject of your dissertation, and not only what you have published but where. Were the articles refereed? Were they published in reputable academic journals? Are the journals discipline-specific, edited and juried by experts in the candidate's field? But I have seen these criteria relaxed time and time again, when these same traditionally trained, nonblack scholars are hired not in the fields in which they were educated but in African American studies. Interestingly enough, the same loosening of standards does not readily occur when black scholars apply for positions as generalists in American or world literature. The educational system is such that it is almost impossible to specialize in African American literature without first being trained in the European and Anglo-American canons, but still this does not keep the powers that be from questioning the preparedness of blacks who apply for jobs as generalists. A dissertation on Toni Morrison or C. L. R. James or W. E. B. Du Bois does not necessarily qualify one as an Americanist, but a thesis on Chaucer or the Brontës or Byron is not an impediment to an appointment as an African Americanist.

Indeed, the question of who should teach what in African American discourse is riddled with ironies and contradictions. Black scholars properly trained in traditional fields—medieval studies, for example—are often assumed or expected to be willing and able to teach black studies. African American studies programs and departments are not supposed to be intellectual ghettos populated exclusively by black scholars, particularly when white scholars want to enter such programs, but the field of African American studies often is treated like a ghetto—the one right and proper place for black intellectuals—when black scholars dare to step out of it, to be medievalists or classicists or Dickensians.

Furthermore, though many white scholars and administrators may theorize African American and black feminist studies as open fields, as acquirable tastes ("You don't have to be one to teach one," as someone put it), this intellectual position is often not reflected in institutional practice. When these same individuals want someone to provide a black reading of their work or black representation on a committee or black resources for their students or information about a particular black author or event, more times than not it is to black faculty that they turn, and not to the white Victorianists they have hired to teach courses in black literature and history.

So here we have another paradox of critical demeanor: the difference between authority and authenticity. Black scholars on predominantly white campuses are rarely authorized simply as scholars. Instead, our racial difference is an authenticating stamp that, as Indira Karamcheti has argued, often casts us in the role of Caliban. Speaking of minority scholars in general, Karamcheti writes:

> We are sometimes seen, it seems to me, as traveling icons of culture, both traditional (as long as we're over there) and nontraditional (when we're right here), unbearably ancient in our folk wisdom and childlike in our infantile need for the sophistication of the West. We are flesh and blood informa-

tion retrieval systems, native informants who demonstrate and act out difference, often with an imperfectly concealed political agenda. We are the local and the regional opposed to the universality of the West, nature to its culture, instinct to its intellect, body to its brain. We are, in fact, encased in the personal and visible facts of our visible selves, walking exemplars of ethnicity and of race.[25]

Walking exemplars of ethnicity and race: this is particularly true for black women scholars on white college campuses where they experience both hypervisibility and superisolation. Unfortunately, icons are not granted tenure automatically; when their canonical year rolls around, these same black female faculty members who have been drawn on as exemplars and used up as role models will find themselves chewed up and spit out because they didn't publish or conform to the rules in some way. Consider for a moment the startling number of brilliant black women scholars who have produced only one book or no book. My operatives (a fancy word for spies) tell me that when the names of these same brilliant black women are raised by search committees or at tenure meetings, the refrain is "We can't hire her; she doesn't have a book. We can't tenure her; she doesn't have a book." Sympathetic white colleagues lament their black colleagues' departures from the university: "Why didn't she just say 'no'?" they ask each other, forgetting all the times they had implored her to say yes, the many occasions on which they sent her students with questions only she could answer or problems only she could solve, or the many instances in which they treated her not like a colleague but like a personal research assistant or native informant.

Given the occult of true black womanhood, to be female and black on today's college campuses is difficult, to be sure. But more troubling still is the fact that commodified, Calibanized black women intellectuals, whose authority as academicians has often been questioned at each turn in their careers, are not supposed to notice the double standard that propels others forward as it keeps them back. For the most part, though, black women in the academy not only have noticed, but we have refused to suffer in silence; our complaints are old news. Many hearts, once warm to the "black woman's plight," her "double jeopardy," her "exceptional burdens," have been frozen by the winters of our discontent. Our grievances have begun to be heard only as "anti-intellectual identity politics" and "proprietary claims." What Houston Baker describes as "black feminist manifestos"—our "admonitions, injunctions, and cautions to those who wish to share the open road"[26]—reveal us to be, even to our most supportive colleagues, small-minded, mean-spirited, and downright petty.

My point is that for many of us, for many black women scholars, questioning the race, ethnicity, culture, and credentials of those authorized to write *our* histories and to teach *our* literature is anything but petty. It is a concern rising from the deepest recesses of who we are in relation to where we live and work. Black women have pioneered a field that, even after more than two decades, remains marginalized within the university, regardless of the popularity of both the field and its black women practitioners. Our at once precarious and overdetermined positions in the academy and our intimate knowledge of social, intellectual, and academic history prompt us not simply to guard our turf, as often accused, but to discipline *our* field, to preserve its integrity and our own.

I have emphasized *our* in order to problematize the possessiveness of our disciplinary concerns. For no matter how compelling, the sense of personal stake that permeates the scholarship by black women about black women just may be an aspect of the insider/outsider quandary for which African American women academics have to take responsibility. It may be time for us to interrogate in new and more clinical ways our proprietary relationship to the field many of us continue to think of as our own.

Such internal review presents its own problem, however. To claim privileged access to the lives and literature of African

American women through what we hold to be the shared experiences of our black female bodies is to cooperate with our own commodification, to buy from and sell back to the dominant culture its constitution of our essentialized identity. On the other hand, to relinquish claim to the experiences of the black body and to confirm its study purely as discourse, simply as a field of inquiry equally open to all, is to collaborate in our own objectification. We become objects of study where we are authorized to be the story, but have no special claim to decoding that story. We can be, but someone else gets to tell us what we mean.

This conundrum operates, of course, in realms beyond such either-or options. But how to find the middle ground, that happier medium? How do we negotiate an intellectually charged space for experience in a way that is not totalizing and essentializing—a space that acknowledges the constructedness of and the differences within our lived experiences while at the same time attending to the inclining, rather than the declining, significance of race, class, culture, gender, and sexuality?

I Once Was Blind, But Now I See

By and large, it is only those who enjoy the privileges of white skin who can hold matters of race at arm's length. The white theorist Jane Gallop, for instance, can say that "race only posed itself as an urgent issue to me in the last couple of years,"[27] but race always has been an urgent issue for Mary Helen Washington, Barbara Christian, and Barbara Smith—indeed for most black feminist critics. Gallop can say that she didn't feel the need to discuss race until the focus of her work shifted from French poststructuralist theory to American feminist literary criticism. But Gayatri Spivak and other third-world women know only too well the fallacies and consequences of treating race as something only other (nonwhite) people own and racism as a problem peculiar to the United States. As Spivak writes: "In the matter of race-sensitive analysis, the chief problem of

American feminist criticism is its identification of racism as such with the constitution of racism in America. Thus, today I see the object of investigation to be not only the history of 'Third World Women' or their testimony but also the production, through the great European theories, often by way of literature, of the colonial object."[28]

The colonial object is furthered not only by the canonical literature of the west, but also by would-be oppositional feminists who continue to see whiteness as so natural, normative, and unproblematic that racial identity is a property only of the nonwhite. Unless the object of study happens to be the othered, race is set outside immediate consideration, at once extratextual and extraterrestrial. Despite decades of painful debate, denial, defensiveness, and color-consciousness raising, "as a woman" in mainstream feminist discourse all too often continues to mean "as a white woman." The philosopher Elizabeth Spelman calls this thoroughly internalized myopia the "Trojan horse of feminist ethnocentrism."[29] Indeed, for women of color who are asked to prove their feminism by placing gender before race, the exclusionary ethnocentrism of such innocent constructions as "women and minorities" is both as hollow and as loaded as the Greeks' wooden horse.

But there is a somewhat more convoluted point to make here. In the same conversation referred to above, Jane Gallop says that African American women have become for her what French men used to be: the people she feels inadequate in relation to and tries hardest to please in her writing. This fear of black feminists "is not just idiosyncratic," Gallop believes—not just hers alone—but a shared anxiety among white women academics. She traces her own awareness of this anxiety to what she calls a "non-encounter" with the black feminist Deborah McDowell, who teaches at the University of Virginia, where Gallop once gave a talk: "I had hoped Deborah McDowell would come to my talk: she was there, she was the one person in the audience that I was really hoping to please."[30] Gallop goes on to explain that in her lecture she read from the manuscript that became *Around 1981: Academic Feminist Literary Theory* (1992), after which someone in the audience asked if she was discussing any black feminist anthologies in her study. "I answered no and tried to justify it, but my justifications rang false in my ears," she replies, continuing:

> Some weeks later a friend of mine showed me a letter from McDowell which mentioned my talk and said that I was just doing the same old thing, citing that I was not talking about any books edited by black women. I obsessed over McDowell's comment until I decided to add a chapter on Pryse and Spillers's *Conjuring*. I had already vowed not to add any more chapters out of fear that I would never finish the book. As powerful as my fear of not finishing is, it was not as strong as my wish for McDowell's approval. For McDowell, whom I do not know, read black feminist critic.

Gallop ends her commentary on what might be called "the influence of anxiety" by noting that McDowell ("read black feminist critic") has come to occupy the place of Jacques Lacan in her psyche in much the same way that "emphasis on race has replaced for [her] something like French vs. American feminism."

It is interesting that while she wanted McDowell's approval, like the white child who insults its mammy one moment and demands a hug the next, Gallop seemed to expect approval without having to do the one thing most likely to win it: include McDowell and other black women scholars in the category of feminist theorists or treat black feminist critics as colleagues to be respected, not feared.

Gallop's confessional narrative—and McDowell's nonspeaking part in it—is troubling. Among other things, these remarks seem to exoticize, eroticize, anomalize, and masculinize (if not demonize) Deborah McDowell and the whole category of "black feminist critic." Just what are the implications of conflating white French men and black American women as thorns in the side of white feminists, as Father Law? Gallop's transference is all the more vexed because she and her collaborators define "the men"—them—as "the enemy" throughout their conversation. In fact, as Nancy Miller puts it, where feminist criticism and French male theorists meet, the result is a "David and Goliath thing, with little Jane Gallop from Duluth taking out her slingshot to use on the great man."[31]

Not-so-little (academically speaking) Jane Gallop wields words like a slingshot; but McDowell, daunting as her scholarly accomplishments are, is no Goliath. There is a very different power relation at work. McDowell, whom I believe Gallop means to honor, is actually diminished by a narrative that casts her somewhere between monster and mammy: demanding, demeaning, impossible to please, but at the same time possessing irresistible custodial power and exotic allure as the larger-than-life racial other.

I rush to add that mammy is my metaphor, not Gallop's. There is nothing in Gallop's commentary that defines McDowell as anything other than "black feminist critic"—nothing that describes her work or explains why she looms so large in Gallop's psyche while writ so small in her text. McDowell, the black feminist critic, is never anything other than *the other* in "Criticizing Feminist Criticism." Race enters the conversation of these three white feminists only through the referenced bodies of objectified black women, and only at those moments when the speakers tally their sins of omission against women of color and their irritation at being chastised or, as they say, trashed for those exclusions.

Spurred by McDowell's criticism, Jane Gallop did indeed add the Pryse and Spillers anthology *Conjuring* to her study of feminist theory, with interesting results. Provocative if tentative, Gallop's critique is most incisive where it attends to the tensions between the different organizing principles set out in the anthology's introduction and afterword. Her study is, for me, most engaging where it attempts to explain that *Conjuring* comes with its own deconstruction.

As Gallop reads it, Marjorie Pryse's introduction argues for a continuum of black women writers—a single, unified tradition rooted in magic, folk wisdom, and "ancient power." Hortense Spillers's afterword, on the other hand, emphasizes cross-currents and discontinuities—differences within a tradition that is itself always in flux. Gallop concludes that Pryse frames and Spillers reframes. Even as Spillers's afterword turns the reader's expectations inside out, Pryse's introduction

> corresponds to and evokes in the reader, at least in the white
> female academic, a fantasy which orients our reading of black
> women. I want the conjure woman; I want some ancient
> power that stands beyond the reaches of white male culture.
> I want black women as the idealized and exoticized alternative
> to European high culture. I want some pure outside and am
> fool enough to think I might find it in a volume published by
> Indiana University Press, with full scholarly apparatus.[32]

This is a difficult passage to digest, especially when the author later admits that she was disappointed that the book was so academic and that she had attributed its particularly erudite essays, with their classical allusions, to critics she imagined to be white. Surely Gallop does not mean what she seems to say here. Is she really admitting in print that she expected a critical anthology subtitled *Black Women, Fiction, and Literary Tradition*—a book edited by two university professors, one of whom has long been regarded as a dean of black feminist criticism—to be other than scholarly, literate, and sophisticated?

To be fair, I think Gallop's tone is meant to be ironic, to point out—and maybe to poke fun at—the essentializing fantasies of "the white female academic" who desires the other to be other, who brings to the text of the other a different set of assumptions, who expects to leave high theory behind when she goes slumming in low culture. Hers is a dangerous strategy, but it seems to be popular among white readers of "black texts," who feel compelled to supplement their criticism with exposés of their former racism (or sexism) in a kind of I-once-was-blind-but-now-I-see way. (It worked for the composer of "Amazing Grace," a re-formed slave trader.) I will have more to say about this strategy in a moment, but for now I want to linger over what is for me more a critique of "the white female academic" than of *Conjuring*. Gallop is subtly telling us that she, as a white woman reader, wanted to find in this black book the exotic black female other, a "new delight," the "spice" to liven up the dull dish of western culture she usually consumes. "Since I am a white academic," she writes, "what sort of fantasy not only renders those attributes contemptible but, from an imagined identification with some righteous outside, allows me to cast them as aspersions on others?" In this instance, Gallop's exoti-cizing movements are not entirely unselfconscious, as they seem to be in "Criticizing Feminist Criticism." As her self-reflective question suggests, her essay is underpinned by an implicit critique of the primitivist expectations that "the white female academic" (I would be more generous and say *some* white female academics) brings to the reading of texts by or about black women.

Even more interesting, however, is Gallop's contention that Pryse's introduction evokes those desires in the reader. She says that reading *Conjuring* for a second time, even knowing that Spillers's corrective essay lay ahead, she still nearly gave in to the introduction's romantic vision of black female folk. "In this chapter I wanted to transmit this illusory take on the anthol-ogy," Gallop writes, "because I consider this illusion central to *our* reading of black women. *We* must confront *our* wish to find this ancient power, this pure outside of academic culture, be-fore *we* deconstruct or correct *our* illusion."[33] In other words, the reader needs to absorb Pryse's framing before Spillers's reframing can take effect.

I'm not quite sure how this follows: why do we need this critical *felix culpa*, this happy slip into what Gallop describes as the folk fantasies of Pryse before *we* can be rescued by the refined vision of Spillers? Perhaps my failure to follow Gallop's logic here stems from her use of "we" and "our," which is at least as problematic as my own. I am not part of her "we," and she is not part of mine. Pryse's introduction did not evoke in me as a reader the kind of desires Gallop evidently assumes it evokes in her universal "we."

What happens if we add to Gallop's notion of the framing/reframing, idealizing/realizing, "good cop/bad cop" routine of the coeditors the fact that Marjorie Pryse is white and Hortense Spillers is black? What does it mean, then, that Spillers both brings up the rear, has the last word, and "deconstructs or corrects" not only Pryse's romantic vision of a black female folk but the primitivist expectations of "the white female academic"? Can one correct where there has been no error? Perhaps because she does not quite dare to play critical hardball with those she seems to take to be two black feminist critics, Gallop bends over backward to soft-pedal the very ideological disjuncture she has so astutely identified. If the coeditors are simply playing out a well-rehearsed routine, as Gallop concludes, why has Pryse positioned herself as the essentializing, idealizing white woman academic and left the corrective black feminist criticism to Spillers?

Gallop's reading of editorial matters in *Conjuring* unwittingly punctuates my point about the dangers of a critical mode that demeans its subject in the very act of analyzing it. It is of course no better for me to use Gallop (or Pryse) as a metonym for white feminist critics than it is for Gallop to use Deborah McDowell. Yet the wide-eyed illusions Gallop attributes to Pryse's introduction and the myopia of her own remarks in "Criticizing Feminist Criticism" demonstrate precisely why it remains so difficult for some black feminists to entrust the texts of our familiar to the critical caretaking of white women (and men) for whom black women are newly discovered foreign bodies, perpetually other.

The Driving Miss Daisy Crazy Syndrome

Yet. Still. And but. If a Ph.D. in English literature is not a title deed to the African American text, neither is black skin. Romantic fantasies of an authentic, cohesive, magical, ancient, all-knowing black female folk are certainly not unique to white academics. Some might argue that the issue is not simply the color or culture of the scholar but the kind, quality, and cultural competence of the scholarship. The black historian Carter Woodson reportedly welcomed the contributions of white scholars, "so long as they were the products of rigorous scholarship and were not contaminated by the venom of racial bias."[34] Unfortunately, biases are ideologically inscribed and institutionally reproduced and are not easily put aside—not even by the most sensitive and the most well-intentioned among us. I think, for example, of Adrienne Rich.

Long a fan of Rich's poetry, I was rather late in coming to her prose. *Of Woman Born: Motherhood as Experience and Institution* (1986), originally published in 1976, was more than a dozen years old before I gave myself the pleasure of reading it. For once, though, my timing couldn't have been better: I discovered this essential book at a critical moment in my life and in the development of my feminism—on the eve of my fortieth birthday, as I wrestled with the likelihood of never having a child. Rich's brilliant analysis of motherhood as an instrument of patriarchy helped me come to terms with the constructedness of what I had been reared to believe were natural maternal instincts, without which I was no woman. But for all that Rich's book gave me, it also took something away; and that, ironically and perhaps a little unfairly, has come to mean almost as much to me as what it gave.

For a moment in the penultimate chapter of this passionate and painful critique of motherhood, Rich turns her remarks toward the black woman who helped to raise her. To this nameless woman Rich assigns the designation "my Black mother." "My Black mother was 'mine,'" she writes, "only for four years, during which she fed me, dressed me, played with me, watched over me, sang to me, cared for me tenderly and intimately." Rich goes on to describe the physical presence of her black mother, from whom she "learned—*nonverbally*—a great deal about the possibilities of dignity in a degrading situation" (my emphasis). Unaware of the degrading situation she is creating herself, she continues: "When I began writing this chapter I began to remember my Black mother again: her calm, realistic vision of things, her physical grace and pride, her beautiful soft voice. For years, she had drifted out of reach, in my searches backward through time, exactly as the double silence of sexism and racism intended her to do. She was meant to be utterly annihilated."[35]

To the silences of sexism and racism Rich adds a third: the silence (and the blindness) of feminism. Like Jane Gallop wanting to praise Deborah McDowell, Adrienne Rich no doubt means to honor the woman who cared for her as a child. But the flow of her prose should not disguise the paternal arrogance of her words or mask the annihilating effect of her claim on the being she resurrects as "my Black mother." Silent and nameless in Rich's book, "my Black mother" has no identity of her own and, in fact, does not exist beyond the nurture she gave exclusively to the young Adrienne.

"'Childless' herself, she *was* a mother," Rich writes of her objectified subject. Her attempt to thrust motherhood on a childless black domestic worker is all the more ironic because of what she claims for all women in the introduction to the anniversary edition of the book: "the claim to personhood; the claim to share justly in the products of our labor, not to be used merely as an instrument, a role, a womb, a pair of hands or a back or a set of fingers; to participate fully in the decisions of our workplace, our community; to speak for ourselves, in our own right."[36] Even in the midst of her own extended criticism of the objectification of women as mothers, Rich has objectified someone she can see only in the possessive case. "My Black mother" is a role, a pair of hands; her function is to "nonverbally" instruct the white child in the ways of the world, even as she cannot speak "in [her] own right."[37]

The child may be father of the man in poetry, but frequently when white intellectuals reminisce about blacks from their past, it is black mammy (metaphorically speaking, even where the mammy figure is a man) who takes the ignorant white infant into enlightenment. Often as the youthful, sometimes guilty witness to the silent martyrdom of the older other, the privileged white person inherits a wisdom, an agelessness, even a racelessness that entitles him or her to the raw materials of another's life and culture but, of course, not to the other's condition.

Such transformative moves often occur in the forewords, afterwords, rationales, and apologia white scholars affix to their scholarly readings of the black other—discussions that just may protest too much, suggesting a somewhat uneasy relationship between author and subject. These prefaces acknowledge the "outsider" status of the authors—their privileged positions as white women or as men—even as they insist on the rightness of their entry into the fields of black literature and history.

Gerda Lerner offers such a rationale in her preface to *Black Women in White America:* "Black people at this moment in history need above all to define themselves autonomously and to interpret their past, their present and their future." Having called upon the black physician to heal her/himself, Lerner then goes on to explain her own presence in the operating room:

> Certainly, historians who are members of the culture, or subculture, about which they write will bring a special quality to their material. Their understanding and interpretation is apt to be different from that of the outsider. On the other hand, scholars from outside a culture have frequently had a more challenging vision than those closely involved in and bound by their own culture. Both angles of vision are complementary in arriving at the truth about the past and in finding out "what actually happened."[38]

A more challenging vision? Why does the perspective of the white scholar reading "the black experience" represent a more challenging vision?

Lerner is not alone in prefacing her work with such a claim. I am reminded of the opening chapter of John Callahan's *In the African-American Grain: Call-and-Response in Twentieth-Century Black Fiction.* Here Callahan takes us on a sentimental journey through his Irish American youth, which was affected not only by his being likened to niggers—"Do you know the definition of an Irishman?" the eight-year-old Callahan is asked by a much bigger Italian boy. "'A Nigger turned inside-out.'"—but also by the black male protectors who taught him "a great deal about the hard work of becoming a man." The teaching tools used by one of these guardians—Bill Jackson, chauffeur for the insurance company at which Callahan worked while in college—include a "prolonged silent challenge" after Callahan calls him a black bastard and his "trickster's way" of teaching certain lessons.[39]

Like Adrienne Rich, Callahan describes his black guide as "silent," even as he credits the chauffeur with teaching him many things "essential to [his] own evolving voice and story." Indeed Bill Jackson, the stereotypical black trickster, remains silent as he is used by Callahan to claim not only his own Irish American voice but entitlement to African American fictions of voice: fictions that "connect and reconnect generations of Americans—African-American, yes and preeminently, but all others too, Irish-Americans like me, for instance—with those past and present oral traditions behind our evolving spoken and written voices."

Here again, to my mind, a critical posturing that means to celebrate a literature demeans it. Callahan's words suggest that we are all brothers not only under the skin but under the book jacket. The white scholar understands "the African-American experience" not in its own right, not on its own terms, but because he can make it like his own. With his voice he can translate another's silence. Bill Jackson's silence is telling, but so too is his profession. It is altogether fitting that Jackson is a chauffeur, for indeed it all invokes what I call the *Driving Miss Daisy* syndrome: an intellectual sleight of hand that transforms power and race relations to make best friends out of driver and driven, master and slave, boss and servant, white boy and black man.

When Callahan overhears the company vice-president lumping together Irish and African Americans as "contemptible, expendable lower caste," he wishes for the strength and skill of a black football player he admires to help him speak up for himself (though apparently not for the other contemptibles). "My fate linked to African-Americans by that Yankee bank officer," Callahan writes, "I became more alert and sympathetic to black Americans my own age and younger who, though cursed, spat upon, and beaten, put their lives and voices on the line to uphold the law of the land and integrate public schools in the South."

Am I to applaud this declaration of allegiance and understanding? No, the claim of fellow feeling and universality—of linked fates and shared voice—makes me profoundly angry and mars my reading of what is actually a fine book. In the end, Callahan's personal narrative, like Rich's, takes symbolic wealth from the martyred, romanticized black body but retains the luxury of ignoring its material poverty. Twenty-five years later, John Callahan is a university professor while, as he tells us in his introduction, Roy Fitch—the protective black mailroom manager under whom he once worked—"looks after" a building near the "plebeian end" of the town green. If we peel away the euphemisms, will we find that Fitch, former mailroom manager, is now a janitor or a security guard for a building near the rundown section of town? Intent as he is on using Fitch to tell his own success story, Callahan does not comment on the historical irony of their relative positions. Nor does he grasp the implications of his own storytelling. "Don't climb no mountain on my back," he recalls Fitch saying to him years before, in response to his awkward attempt to apologize for yet another racial slur. Had Callahan understood the significance of Fitch's words—were he as good at interpreting speech as silence—he could not have written the introduction he did.

However troubling Rich's and Callahan's apologies may be to me as a black woman reader, the white scholar Missy Dehn Kubitschek acknowledges an indebtedness to the latter: "My admiration for 'Who You For?,'" she writes in the preface to *Claiming the Heritage: African-American Women Novelists and History*, "led me to consider voicing my own simultaneously social and psychic travels as a prelude to this study of African-American women's novels."[40]

Following Callahan's lead, Kubitschek opens her study with "A Personal Preface," in which she offers a first-hand account (complete with family history) of how she as a white woman and a British Victorianist came to write a book about African American women novelists. Briefly told, one of the principal players in her disciplinary conversion was her grandmother, a long-time armchair racist, who changed her mind after watching a television program about the "dangerous urban black ghetto" of East St. Louis. Mediated through the medium of television, urban blacks became objects of pity for Mrs. Dehn rather than fear. The possibilities of her grandmother's "impossible" change of heart at such an advanced age were "seismic" for Kubitschek, who was a graduate student at the time and who found in that conversion the seeds of her own.

But other transformative encounters lay ahead for Kubitschek, which not only helped her to get over her family's racism but over her own as well. Arriving early for work one morning in the basement office of the English department, Kubitschek was terrified first by hearing a male voice and then by the sudden appearance of a black man. Reading the horror writ large across her face, the man, a construction worker apparently also early on site for renovating the building, "quickly" and "quietly" explained that he just wanted to use the phone. "Of course, I had been afraid before I had seen that he was black," Kubitschek writes. "Rape is always a threat to women, always a possibility." But seeing his black skin heightened her fear, she admits, and revealed her racism. Because she had recently read Richard Wright's "Big Boy Leaves Home," she knew the historical implications of her reaction. "'Race' ceased to be something that had constructed other people, especially blacks," as she began to understand herself as a racial as well as a gendered being.

Rape is truly a threat to women, particularly to a woman alone with a man. Black man, white man, green man from Mars, I too would have been afraid in Kubitschek's shoes. Her fear feels more legitimate to me than the white liberal guilt that no doubt leads her to call her fear racism and to apologize for it in a preface to a book about African American women writers. Through yet another troubling sleight of text, Kubitschek's articulated awareness of her former racism becomes the authorizing agent behind her strange metamorphosis from British Victorianist to African Americanist.

I know I should be more patient, more sisterly, more respectful of other people's discoveries. I know my bad attitude comes from what in this instance might be called the arrogance of black privilege: after all, I—whose earliest childhood memories include finding a snake in our mailbox shortly after we moved into an all-white neighborhood and being called "nigger" on my first day at school—did not learn my racial consciousness from reading Richard Wright's "Big Boy Leaves Home" as an adult. But I mean my criticism as a kindness. Perhaps if I can approximate in words what is so offensive about these *Driving Miss Daisy* confessionals, I will do the field and all those who want to work in it a genuine favor. Perhaps if I can begin to delineate the difference between critical analysis that honors the field and guilty rhetoric that dishonors it, I can contribute something positive to the future production of scholarship on African American women. Unfortunately, the words don't come easily and the heart of what's the matter is a difficult place to reach. How do you tell people who don't get it in the first instance that it is only out of the arrogance of white privilege or male prerogative that they find it an honor for a black woman to be proclaimed their black mother or their black friend or their black guardian or their black conscience?

It would be a mistake, however, to imply that these gestures are solely the product of white privilege. For my money, the occult of true black womanhood has generated few more troubling renderings of African American women writers and critics than that offered by Houston Baker in *Workings of the Spirit: The Poetics of Afro-American Women's Writing*. Having largely ignored black women as cultural producers throughout his long and distinguished career, Baker takes them up in *Workings*. And like Missy Dehn Kubitschek, for whom the writing of African American women is a kind of survival kit,[41] Baker tells us in his conclusion that a traumatic experience led him to seek solace in the "expressive resistances of Afro-American women's talking books."

The texts of Afro-American women writers became mine and my friend's harrowing but sustaining path to a new, common, and, we thought, empowering discourse and commitment. To "victim," in my friend's semantics, was added the title and entitlement "survivor." Are we not all only that? Victim/Survivors?[42]

Both Kubitschek and Baker seem unaware of the ways in which their survival-kit claims to black texts can reinscribe African American women writers and their characters as magnanimous mammies who not only endure, like Faulkner's Dilsey, but whose primary function is to teach others to do the same. Though Baker is certainly entitled to tell his story, using personal tragedy to claim entitlement to the texts of black women makes me distrust not his cultural competence, perhaps, but his gender sensibility—his ability to handle with care the sacred text of me and mine.

But I was made suspicious of *Workings of the Spirit* long before I got to its conclusion. Baker also includes an introduction that calls attention to himself as outsider. He begins by acknowledging the prior claims and the "cautious anxieties" of black feminist critics such as Barbara Smith, Barbara Christian, and

Mary Helen Washington, who mined the "provinces of Afro-American women's expressivity" that he is just now entering. A "blackmale" scholar "will find cause to mind his steps in a demanding territory," he asserts, his province/metropole metaphor confirming him in the very role he wants most to avoid—that of colonizing, come-lately "blackmale" critic. Such diction is a small example of what seems to me a major problem with *Workings of the Spirit:* the hierarchical relation between what he inevitably treats as master (male) and minor (female) narrative traditions.

Rather than building on the work of black women scholars who excavated the field, Baker either ignores or dismisses what he implies is their historical (as opposed to theoretical) feminist criticism in favor of his own masculinist theorizing. Male figures such as Douglass, Du Bois, Wright, and Ellison are the oracles against which black women's expressivity and cultural fidelity are measured. In *Workings*'s third chapter, for instance, to get to Baker's reading of Morrison's *Sula,* you first have to wade through thirty pages on Wright. The attention to Wright (and other male artists and intellectuals) is justified, Baker argues, because "classic Afro-American male texts" provide a touchstone from which "to proceed by distinctions" in exploring the provinces of black female expressivity.

Like much of the new "new scholarship" that has come out of the occult of true black womanhood, Baker's book fails to live up to its own postmodern, deconstructive principles. It achieves neither inversion nor subversion; black women writers and the black feminist critics who read them remain fetishized bodies set against analytical white or superior male minds. As objects of investigation in such studies, black women are constructed in terms of their difference from or (in the name of sisterhood) similarity to the spectator, whether the spectator is a black male theorist or a white feminist critic. In other words, the black woman is made only more other by the male theorist or by the "white female academic" who views the subject from a position of unrelinquished authority.

Baker is of course free to disagree with black women scholars (as we frequently do with one another), but his failure to value their critical insights undermines his effort to enter into dialogue. His privileging of male subjects in a book about black women writers becomes an act of silencing and makes his text the victim of its own intentional phallacy: his stated wish to avoid appropriating the work and images of African American women through a "blackmale" gaze.

His essential and, I think, essentializing metaphors—black women as "departed daughters" and "spirit workers"—together with the uncontextualized photographs of black women interspersed throughout the book, raise questions about the gaze, about specularization and objectification, that Baker does not address or, I suspect, even see. This is too bad, especially after Mae Henderson—one of the black feminist critics Baker faintly praises for her "fine theorizing"—called his attention to the problem in criticizing an earlier essay that was the prototype for *Workings of the Spirit*. The danger, she warned, "is not only that of essentializing but of reinforcing the most conventional constructs of (black) femininity." Henderson was troubled in particular by the "*specularity* of [Baker's] rather spectacular theory" of black female spirituality. She cautioned him to rethink his treatment of black women in terms that would not objectify and idealize them.[43]

Despite Henderson's incisive critique and her pointed admonition, *Workings of the Spirit* continues the specularization of black women that its prototypical essay began. The book's complementary phototext, in fact, evokes precisely what Henderson called "the male activity of scopophilia." Largely unremarked except for occasional captioned quotation from Baker's written words, the images of black women interspersed throughout the text objectify graphically those whom the book objectifies linguistically. But in another example of Baker's strategic deployment of women, this objectification is made *okay* by the author's claim that the phototext is the handiwork not of senior blackmale theorist Houston Baker but of junior female scholars

Elizabeth Alexander and Patricia Redmond. This is Baker's final point:

> The phototext is the artistry of two young scholars. Their complementary text is a rich enhancement of the present work, and I cannot thank Elizabeth Alexander and Patricia Redmond enough for their collaboration. It seems to me that the intertextuality represented by their effort makes the present work more engaging than it would otherwise have been. My initial idea was that such a text would comprise a type of countercurrent of signification, soliciting always my own words, qualifying their "maleness." What emerged from the labors of Redmond and Alexander, however, is a visualization of an Afro-American women's poetics. Eyes and events engage the reader/viewer in a solicitous order of discourse that asks: "Who reads here?"[44]

If these photos could indeed ask such a question, their answer would probably be: "A man." Baker wants the photos to speak for themselves of "the space, place, and time of Afro-American women," but it is unclear how they can do that in the midst of what is *his* project. Whose project the phototext is becomes even clearer when we know that Alexander and Redmond were graduate students assigned by Baker to collect pictures. The image presented as the "parting shot" of the book is of a young black woman, her mouth open wide as if in a scream. I wonder what it means that the black woman depicted in midscream is literally, physically, clinically mute.

I am not quite certain where to go from here. I find myself oddly drawn to (gulp) William Faulkner. The griefs of great literature, Faulkner said in his Nobel Prize acceptance speech, must grieve on universal bones. I realize that I've heard this before, and not just from Faulkner. The self-recognition generated by the literature of the ennobled other is the essence of Callahan's professed link to African American "fictions of voice" and the medium of Baker's and Kubitschek's claims to the texts of black women. And they are not alone. As Hazel

Carby points out, women's studies programs and literature departments have often used reductive readings of black women (either long-suffering or triumphantly noble) to fill in the gaps in their otherwise Eurocentric or Anglocentric curricular offerings. "In spite of the fact that the writing of black women is extraordinarily diverse, complex, and multifaceted," she writes, "feminist theory has frequently used and abused this material to produce an essential black female subject for its own consumption." Carby also suggests that for many white students and faculty the black female subject and cultural texts by and about African Americans have become "fictional substitutes" for any kind of "sustained social or political relationships with black people."[45]

This is precisely the function that black writers such as Toni Morrison, Alice Walker, and Gayl Jones seem to serve for three white academics, who claim to identify closely with the depictions of physical and psychic abuse in these authors' fiction. As they explain: "We, as white feminists, are drawn to black women's visions because they concretize and make vivid a system of oppression." Indeed, they continue, "it has not been unusual for white women writers to seek to understand their oppression through reference to the atrocities experienced by other groups."[46] For these feminists, as for Baker and Kubitschek, the lure of black women's fiction is, at least in part, its capacity to teach them how to endure, how to understand not the complex experiences of black women but their own.

Is this use of black women's texts a bad thing? If Faulkner is right—if it is the writer's duty to help humankind endure by reminding us of our capacity for courage and honor and hope and pride and compassion and sacrifice and survival—black women writers have done the job very well. The griefs of African American women indeed seem to grieve on universal bones—"to concretize and make vivid a system of oppression." But it also seems that in order to grieve universally, to be concrete, to have larger meaning—the flesh on these bones must always be white or male.

This, then, is the final paradox: to be valid—to be true—black womanhood must be legible as white or male; the texts of black women must be readable as maps, indexes to someone else's experience, subject to a seemingly endless process of translation and transference. Under the cult of true black womanhood, the colored body, as Cherríe Moraga writes, is "thrown over a river of tormented history to bridge the gap,"[47] to make connections that enable scholars working in exhausted fields to cross over into the promised land.

The trouble is that, as Moraga points out, bridges get walked on over and over again. To be a bridge—walked on and passed over, used up and burned out, publishing while perishing—characterizes the condition of many black women scholars. Neither academia nor mainstream feminism has paid much attention to the crisis of black female intellectuals. But the issue is much on the minds of African American women, caught as we are in the throes of a repressive political climate that would lay the nation's ills on the backs of poor black "welfare queens," on the one hand, and overeducated elite black "quota queens," on the other. Even as welfare mothers are told to go out and get jobs, working women are blamed for the disintegration of the home and the erosion of family values that are figured as the real cause of crime and all other social problems. The status of black women in America seems all the more tenuous in light of certain "events" such as the Thomas-Hill hearings, the media-fed campaigns to discredit Lani Guinier and former Surgeon General Joycelyn Elders, and the recent deaths of a number of black female scholars and artists, including Audre Lorde (Hunter College), Sylvia Boone (Yale), Phyllis Wallace (MIT), and Toni Cade Bambara.

So serious are these issues that the lot of black women in the university became the subject of a national conference held at MIT in January 1994. Called "Black Women in the Academy: Defending Our Name, 1894–1994," this conference, the first of its kind, drew over two thousand women—most of them black—from across the country. Robin Kilson and Evelynn Hammonds, the conference organizers, said that they were overwhelmed by the response to their initial call for papers. Expecting to host a small gathering of perhaps two hundred people, they found themselves bombarded by hundreds of abstracts, letters, faxes, and phone calls from black women anxious for a forum in which to discuss the hypervisibility, emotional quarantine, and psychic violence of their precarious positions in academia.[48]

I do not mean to imply that all black women scholars see themselves as what Hurston called "tragically colored," but I think it safe to say that these testimonies are a plaintive cry from black women academics who see themselves consumed by exhaustion, depression, loneliness, and a higher incidence of such killing diseases as hypertension, lupus, cancer, diabetes, and obesity. But it also seems to me that Jane Gallop's anxieties about African American women, Nancy Miller's fear that there is no position from which a middle-class white woman can speak about race without being offensive, and Houston Baker's desire for dialogue with black women scholars are also plaintive cries. In different ways and with different consequences, we all experience the pain and disappointment of failed community.

As much as I would like to end on a positive note, I have little faith that this generation of scholars—black and nonblack, male and female—will succeed in solving these problems. We are too set in our ways, too alternately defensive and offensive, too much the products of the white heterosexist society that has reared us and the Eurocentric educational system that has trained us. Training may be the critical factor, however—the only way out of the occult of true black womanhood—in terms of both the cultural competence we must bring to the field and the professional guidance we must give to the students we bring into the field. If ever there came a day when all scholars were forced by the systems that educate them to know as much about "minority discourses" as scholars of color are required to know about so-called dominant cultures, perhaps black women would no longer be exotic commodities, and African American studies would indeed be everybody's business as usual.

Discourse and Dat Course: Postcoloniality and Afrocentricity

After the Egyptian and Indian, the Greek and Roman, the Teuton and Mongolian, the Negro is a sort of seventh son, born with a veil, and gifted with second-sight in this American world,—a world which yields him no true self-consciousness, but only lets him see himself through the revelation of the other world. It is a peculiar sensation, this double-consciousness, this sense of always looking at one's self through the eyes of others, of measuring one's soul by the tape of a world that looks on in amused contempt and pity.

—W. E. B. Du Bois, *The Souls of Black Folk* (1903)

For every action there is an equal and opposite reaction. For every doubly conscious racial or ethnic other constructed by institutions, there is a self attempting to assert its subjectivity. For many intellectuals, asserting a racial or national self has meant claiming as "familiar" everything African, Indian, or Caribbean and expelling as "foreign" all things British, French, Spanish, or even Anglo-American. Yet centuries of close encounters of the Columbian kind have produced a world out of joint, and often it is the would-be familiar that is foreign and the self that is alien. Black Americans, many of whom will never see Dakar or Lagos, choose African names from books (most likely published in the United States or Britain) in unknowing contradiction of the very cultural traditions they wish to celebrate.

In many traditional West African societies—the Yoruba of Nigeria, for instance—naming is an essential postnatal ritual, a communal event that generally takes place after birth, after a child has been presented to a waiting extended family, which only then christens the infant in ceremonial splendor and cultural specificity. For Africans whose names were so chosen, the would-be Afrocentric American tradition of christening a child *in utero*—with the aid of a book of African names—is close to sacrilege. Much the same is true for the Afrocentric practice whereby black adults rename themselves. Ghanaian names are especially popular among African Americans seeking to reclaim what slavery stripped them of; but for many Ghanaians the idea of an adult man born on a Monday naming himself Kofi (Friday) rather than Kojo (Monday) is at once laughable and lamentable.

This misnaming and other efforts to reclaim a homeland reinscribe our cultural dislocation. We sport Afros and don dreadlocks as visible signs of our essential Africanness, unaware that in most contemporary African societies, these "specifically diasporean" styles would identify us with the west, with the first world and not the third.[1]

Even the language in which we write at once underscores our alienation from "home" and our arrival within the academy; it is not in Hindi or Yoruba that we contemplate our postcoloniality and Afrocentricity, but in the fine and proper English of the colonizer. What we seek is a precolonial connection; what we theorize is a postcolonial condition; what we're stuck with is a perennial colonial contradiction. Illiterate in the languages of the homeland, we must use the master's tongue to talk our way out of his house—even when that house is on *our* land. As we labor to expel the alien within, our acts of intellectual and political exorcism, however culturally empowering, often produce blindspots that misshape our postcolonial conditions and our Afrocentric ideas.

Ethnic Notions

Afrocentric ideas are everywhere, it seems—from the "African Pride" hair straighteners sold in the "Ethnic Needs" aisle at Super Stop & Shop, to the fake kente placemats available though J.C. Penney's "Afrocentric" catalogue. In academic arenas, Afrocentrism has at times joined forces with multiculturalism in challenging the Eurocentric bent of public education and lobbying for curriculum changes at both the elementary and secondary school levels. In other instances, demands for Afrocentric curricula in urban areas such as Detroit and Milwaukee have led to the establishment of academies devoted exclusively to the education of young black men. When it comes to higher education, the epicenter of Afrocentricism is, indisputably, the African American Studies department at Temple University, home to Molefi Kete Asante—the nation's premier proponent of Afrocentricity (a term he coined)—and over two hundred graduate students.

Because the term has been used to include everything from food and fashion to racial fundamentalism, Afrocentrism has become a hot topic both within and outside the academy. Academic journals have fanned the flames of the increasingly heated debate between black intellectuals such as Henry Louis Gates—head of Afro-American Studies at Harvard—and cultural nationalists like Asante, who heads Temple's African American Studies department. What's at stake in this ideological campaign, most spectators agree, is the very future of black studies.

While academia waits eagerly to see if Gates and Harvard's black intelligentsia can indeed "kick Asante's ass,"[2] the media are busy tracking what they perceive to be the more radical (hence more newsworthy) antics of "loud-mouth extremists" and conspiracy theorists, such as Louis Farrakhan and Khalid Muhammad of the Nation of Islam and Leonard Jeffries of the City University of New York. Indeed, the popular press seems to take special delight in linking academic Afrocentrism of the Asante kind with what it calls the loony theories and antisemitic utterings of the likes of Jeffries, who—in the words of one set of reporters—"seems to believe in a conspiracy to oppress blacks that stretches from classrooms to the Mafia and Jewish movie producers."[3]

Tempting as these topics are, I would rather focus on the increasingly fraught (but less often discussed) relationship between postcoloniality and Afrocentricity as intellectual perspectives, as acclaimed and disclaimed discourses respectively. Occupied with each other, some Afrocentrists and multiculturalists have little noticed that the academy has opened its doors to another oppositional discourse: postcolonial studies. Others have not only noticed; they have begun to fear for their own intellectual lives.

As an African Americanist, I make no claim of neutrality, but I do want to say that I am neither a proponent of Afrocentricity nor an opponent of postcoloniality. My hope is, first, to discuss what these two disciplines have in common as therapeutic antidotes to imperialism and, second, to explore their different deployments within academia. What does it mean, for example, when Afrocentricity is dismissed as methodologically sloppy, anti-intellectual identity politics, while postcoloniality is affirmed as theoretically sophisticated oppositional discourse? The most critical factor in the reception of these two resistance narratives may have more to do with market than with methodology—with the academic merchandising of *different* difference.

If postcoloniality is discourse—an exotic, foreign field whose time has come within the U.S. academy—Afrocentricity is "dat course"—local color (homeboys and homegirls) whose time has come and gone, if indeed it ever was. Blacks are after all, in the words of Richard Wright, America's metaphor. Our otherness has become in some ways too familiar. In American feminist studies, the enslavement and breeding of African women is yesterday's news, like the Doberman biting the mailman. Widow burning, on the other hand, is not simply history; it is story.

Popularizing the Postcolonial

In a special issue of *Social Text*, which, among other things, interrogates such phrases as "third world" and "postcolonial," Ella Shohat defines the latter term as "a new designation for critical discourses which thematize issues emerging from colonial relations and their aftermath."[4] Indira Karamcheti has also taken note of the increasing popularity of all things "postcolonial": postcolonial theory, postcolonial studies, and postcolonial literature. "The stars of postcolonial literary studies shine brightly in the dim skies of academe," Karamcheti writes, citing Edward Said, Gayatri Chakravorty Spivak, Kwame Anthony Appiah, Gauri Viswanathan, Sara Suleri, R. Radhakrishnan, Abdul JanMohamed, and Rey Chow.[5]

Like the presence of these luminary scholars, interest in postcoloniality is everywhere in the academy: in journal articles, including several special issues devoted entirely to postcolonial themes (in *Representations, PMLA, Callaloo,* and *Social Text*); at university presses that have started postcolonial series; in job announcements calling for specialists in postcolonial literary, theoretical, and cultural studies; in learned societies whose annual meetings for the past few years have sponsored panels devoted to postcolonial themes. For many of us who regularly read such publications and attend such conferences, these times have felt more and more like the dawning of a new age.

Although the designation "postcolonial" may be new, the study of power relations between colonizer and colonized is not. In the United States, black intellectuals such as W. E. B. Du Bois, Alexander Crummell, Pauline Hopkins, and Anna Julia Cooper discussed such themes in the late nineteenth and early twentieth centuries. More recently, but still decades before the rise of postcoloniality as an academic discipline, black activists and scholars, writers such as Marcus Garvey, Claude McKay, C. L. R. James, Frantz Fanon, and Aimé Césaire explored and exploded colonial and postcolonial power relations. In current academic theaters, Stuart Hall, Sylvia Wynter, Selwyn Cudjoe, Cedric Robinson, Alex Dupuy, Paget Henry, Paul Gilroy, Hazel Carby, bell hooks, Audre Lorde, Angela Davis, and Cheikh Anta Diop are among the many scholars of African descent who continue to probe the relationship between Prospero and Caliban, metropole and province.

The difference between my list of black scholars and the earlier inventory of Asian postcolonial theorists is a distinction that has inspired at least two kinds of charges from some Afrocentrists: that once again foreigners have taken over *our* field, and that it takes the interest of outsiders to legitimize a discourse of which the academy took little note when it was dominated by diasporic blacks. Although these charges have a certain history, they may not be pertinent to the rise of postcolonial studies. There is at least one other causal relation that Afrocentrism has all but ignored: spontaneous generation, in which postcoloniality (like Afrocentricity) developed as an equal and opposite reaction to the oppressions of imperialism. Postcoloniality is not so much the heir apparent to and beneficiary of other resistance narratives as it is their coincidence—an oppositional discourse with its own history of what Paget Henry calls "discursive insurrection," played out in the texts of native writers throughout the subaltern.[6]

Were I well versed in other "minority literatures," I could no doubt rattle off an impressive list of Indian, Middle Eastern, or Southeast Asian textual insurrectionists. The first-world academy in which so many of us are trained, however, has rarely fostered knowledge of either the non-European self or the foreign other. In attending so narrowly to its own racial and cultural self, Afrocentrism—more correctly, some brands of Afrocentrism—perpetuates the same divide-and-conquer ignorance on which imperialism has depended.

But if Afrocentricity errs in its cultural ethnocentrism, post-coloniality, precisely because it is taken more seriously by the academy, has an even more dangerously myopic relation to the company it keeps and the company that keeps it. Like Afrocentricity, it suffers from a limited perspective that sees its own colonized body in relation to a particular imperial force, even as it claims a global view. Moreover, the academy to which it has become attached has a vested interest in promoting the illusions of grandeur that the very term *postcolonial* suggests. From the ivory tower, conceptualizing a politically correct postcolonial globe makes it easier to get around the fact that much of the world's population lives in conditions that are hardly "postcolonial." This is particularly true of women who, as Anne McClintock notes, "do 2/3 of the world's work, earn 10% of the world's income, and own less than 1% of the world's property."[7] False universals, such as the postcolonial woman, the postcolonial other, the postcolonial condition, and even the postcolonial critic, camouflage the variety of neocolonial circumstances in which masses of people live, work, and theorize. If Afrocentricity has an overdetermined (and some say grossly exaggerated) sense of its own glorious past, the false universals of postcoloniality often obscure both its lineage and its connection to other narratives of marginality.

Postcolonial discourse rises today in the U.S. academy as a more elegant incarnation of what used to be called world literature, third-world literature, Commonwealth studies, or area studies—all contemplations of the exotic, foreign other. As an academic discipline, postcoloniality takes its current preeminence not only from the traditional, often orientalist, and remarkably well-funded area studies it has somewhat eclipsed, but also from the very resistance narratives it seems to threaten: black studies and women's studies, for example. Unlike African American and other local narratives of marginality, postcoloniality is being figured as a universal master narrative containing all difference. "If it continues to be developed as a totalizing narrative cut off from a local place," Indira Karamcheti warns, "it can be used within academia to displace those minority groups whose social struggles for inclusion, empowerment, and representation cleared the space within which postcoloniality operates."[8] Put another way, its ties to poststructuralism and the dissolution of the essential features of many minority discourses make postcoloniality not simply a resistance narrative but a containment strategy.

Karamcheti is not alone in warning of the potential abuses of academic postcoloniality. Noting that some ethnic-studies scholars feel set adrift by the rising tide of postcolonial studies in English departments, Ella Shohat suggests that the term *postcolonial* has received ready institutional endorsement because it enables a "partial containment of the POCs (people of color)." In the North American context, she adds, "one has the impression that the 'post-colonial' is privileged precisely because it seems safely distant from 'the belly of the beast,' the United States."[9] Whereas the critique from African American studies and the alternative worldview from Afrocentricity cut uncomfortably close to home, postcoloniality seems to pose its opposition from a distance—as Gayatri Spivak might say, "in other worlds."

Dislocated Discourses

But postcoloniality is a discourse still in the process of locating itself. It has been taken up by an academy that does not necessarily know what it is. Afrocentricity, by contrast, has been dismissed by the same academy that knows only too well what it is. Despite a current breath of life from Molefi Asante, the Afrocentric idea is hardly a new one. Speaking perhaps reductively, one could say that this effort to read diasporic experiences through reconstituted African ideals, belief systems, and cultural traditions has led other lives as Pan-Africanism, Garveyism, and back-to-Africa-ism in the 1920s, as negritude in the 1930s, and as the black-arts, black-power, and black-is-beautiful movements of the 1960s.

However empowering it may be for some black scholars, Afrocentricity has been spurned not only by much of the white European and Anglo-American academy but also by such leading black intellectuals as Clarence Walker, Cornel West, and Gates. West, for example, defines Afrocentrism as a contemporary brand of black nationalism that is gallant in its focus on "black doings and sufferings," but misguided in its fear of cultural hybridization, its inattention to issues of class, and its retrograde views on gender and sexuality.[10] Barbara Ransby, who sees Afrocentricity as a much misunderstood concept whose very definition is contested, reminds us that cultural nationalists like Asante do not have a monopoly on the term. (Patricia Hill Collins, for one, defines her decidedly black feminist perspective as Afrocentric, though her sociological work bears little resemblance to the male-centered theorizing of Asante.) Ransby rightly credits Asante for his role in forcing the academy to confront its Eurocentrism, but she also details some of the weaknesses in his brand of Afrocentrism, including sexism and homophobia. Analyzing the work of Haki Madhubuti and Na'im Akbar as well, Ransby argues that their brand of Afrocentrism denies the contributions of gay and lesbian activists and ignores the oppression of black women.[11]

Rejected even by what it would take to be "its own," Afrocentricity is a kind of bad-kid ideology within academia, a thankless-child anti-intellectualism that denies daddy, resists paternity, refuses to acknowledge Europe as its great white father. As its very name implies, postcoloniality, by contrast, seems to be a properly indebted, if rebellious, intellectual offspring. Its name announces its relation not to Mother Africa or India or China but to Father Europe, the colonizer without whom there would be neither colonial nor postcolonial. Where Afrocentricity is culturally exclusive and self-centered, postcoloniality is intellectually elastic and decentered. Where the former disdains theory, the latter thrives on it. Where the one is "unembarrassingly black," in the words of Joyce Joyce, the other is black only by default—de fault of being nonwhite.

The nonwhite, no-fault "blackness" of Indian, Bengali, Asian, Arab, Egyptian, and other "brown" postcolonial scholars has proven a boon for the North American academy. For one thing, affirmative action need no longer be an act of contrition. The displacement of cultural and geopolitical difference has enabled an easier diversity, a "black" presence without the historical and political particularities of Spivak's "black blacks." The academy, in effect, gets to eat its chocolate cake and have it too. Among the ingredients it leaves out, however, are racial identity, geopolitical ethnicity, and cultural specificity.

Both Afrocentricity and postcoloniality, it seems to me, have their origins in this hard-to-swallow difference—in an alterity that is at once institutionally promoted and intellectually denied. By this I mean that, on the one hand, the academy fosters a kind of skin trade that has made alterity the bestseller in the intellectual marketplace. On the other hand, it theorizes racial differences in solipsisms that obscure color, class, caste, culture, gender, sexuality, and place. Blackness becomes the metonymic expression of race, and the rainbow coalition is viewed on a dichromatic scale that only sees black and white. Put another way, though race may be a sign of irreducible difference, it also may be a sign of reducible *sameness*—of a homogenization that refuses specificity.[12] Let me clarify the point I'm trying to make by returning to the example of the Indian.

At one point in my research on Barbie dolls, I was in desperate pursuit of Indian Barbie. Dealers, collectors, and salesclerks understood readily enough what I meant when I asked for Eskimo Barbie or Spanish Barbie or Malaysian Barbie or Jamaican Barbie, but when I said I was looking for Indian Barbie, the response was either a question—"American or East Indian?"—or the assumption that I meant the doll Mattel markets as Native American Barbie.

In the continental United States, "Indians" have red skin and live on reservations, where they play bingo, build casinos, and plot to take over white people's land. Columbus discovered and named these people five hundred years ago. Marlon Brando rediscovered them in the 1960s, as did Kevin Costner in the 1990s. Even though it repeats Columbus's blunder, we continue to call these people Indians. Our current use of "Indian" as a synonym both for "native" and for "Native American" replicates the fifteenth- and sixteenth-century usage of the term as a generic designation for "nonwhite"—a misnomenclature that, through the centuries, has given the world Asian, African, Australian, Mexican, Caribbean, Hawaiian, and many varieties of North and South American "Indians." What does this mean for natives of the Indian subcontinent—for people of the Indus—whose own cultural, racial, and geopolitical specificity is denied by this generic use of the name they would call themselves?

For the postcolonial from the jewel in the crown of the British Raj, claiming self—claiming "Indianness"—in the United States begins not only with the assertion of India, the land Columbus did not discover, but with the unnaming of the "Indians," the people he supposedly did. Then, too, there are the multiracial, ethnically variegated inhabitants of the Caribbean, the "West Indians." What are we to make of them? Contemplating all these Indians (something we rarely do in the academy) brings back the silly song I learned in elementary school: "One little, two little, three little Indians." Even if some of them appear without warpaint and tomahawks, three little Indians are at least two too many for intellectual ease and theoretical comfort. First-world academia gets around this problem, it seems to me, by erasing "Indianness" from its lexicon, if not its cultural consciousness. It has largely ignored Columbus's misnamed Indian, except where the discourse of political correctness and romantic notions of native spirituality have necessitated a kind of lip-service to the "Native American."[13] It has translated the multivocality, racial diversity, and ethnic variety of what it calls the West Indian into a monochromatic scale of ubiquitous blackness, ignoring both Indians from India and the native Caribs and Arawaks. The "one little, two little, three little Indians" have been replaced by "the black" or, more recently, "the postcolonial"; that is to say, the same academy that rushed to validate postcoloniality has done away with Indianness. The alterity of the Indian as postcolonial is generic, categorical, locational, but, interestingly enough, not racial or at least not racially specific. Race, it seems, is the proper attribute of black or African people.

In Great Britain, Indians are considered "black," along with Africans, Afro-Caribbeans, and African Americans. In the United States, the racial status of Indians and several other minorities has varied with the political and social agenda of the historical moment. Anthropologically, Indians in India were classified as Caucasians, but when migration to the United States began in the early 1900s, that designation did not necessarily entitle them to the rights and privileges of other white immigrants, particularly naturalization, landownership, and citizenship. In 1922, the Supreme Court in *U.S. v. Thind* ruled that Bhagat Sigh Thind, a high-caste Punjabi, was not eligible for U.S. citizenship because he was not white in the sense intended by the framers of the Constitution. Academically, in this country, the racial status of Indians has been even more ambiguous. I know of more than one institution of higher learning that either by accident, ignorance, or design has augmented its statistics on the recruitment of black professors by counting Indian and other "brown" scholars among its black faculty.

On both sides of the Atlantic, a Eurocentric vision that sees only white and nonwhite translates the object of its intellectual gaze into white and black, where black is the metonym for all racial alterity. Within the U.S. academy, it is blackness, not Indianness, that has racial and cultural currency. Ironically, it is postcoloniality and not Afrocentricity that has intellectual cachet.

Returning to theories of action and reaction, I think the joke may be on the academy. I began by invoking Newton's law of motion to suggest that, for every constructed other, there is a self attempting to assert its subjectivity. Afrocentricity is, in some measure, such a reaction—an attempt to assert a distinctly African racial and cultural subjectivity, a truly black consciousness or an authentically black identity. Unfortunately, this particular effort denies cultural specificity and geopolitical ethnicity and reproduces racial hierarchies (who's blacker than whom) just as the academy does.

The vitriolic exchange in the pages of *New Literary History* (Winter 1987) between Joyce Joyce, on the one hand, and Henry Louis Gates and Houston Baker, on the other, is a glaring case in point. Arguing from an Afrocentric perspective, Joyce accuses Gates and Baker of not being black enough, even as they charge her with being too black. Similar blacker-than-thou politics are at work in Asante's response to Gates's threatened ass-kicking: "I am clear that the aping of whites is the road to neither intellectual respect nor ethical decency. Africans who exhibit confusion about their personal identities cannot hope to be clear about cultural identity."[14] Precisely the point that Gates and other multiculturalists insist on is that culture is not "clear," transhistorical, or one-dimensional—whether the assumed center is Europe or Africa.

Although the empowering premise of Afrocentric methodology offers a challenge to the universality of European paradigms, it does not sufficiently address the question of cultural mediation. Although it acknowledges blacks in the Americas as an African-derived people with their own cultural legacies, it does not adequately consider the degree to which Euro-American culture is intertwined with those around it. Nor does it consider the global implications of the imperialist agenda or what Spivak and others refer to as the colonial object.

"Cultures are not containable," the white deconstructionist Barbara Johnson tells us, and even the terms black and white are fallacious. They "imply a relation of mutual exclusion"—a binarism based on the notion of "pure, unified, and separate traditions"[15]—in the face of what are, I would add, interlocking cultural and linguistic phenomena. But in some Afrocentric circles, my acknowledgment of cultural symbiosis is a kind of heresy likely to place my blackness, like Gates's and Baker's, under suspicion. Many Afrocentrists, perhaps in reaction against notions of hybridity and the encroachments that come with them, have tried to purge themselves and African diasporic discourses of what Larry Neal called the "white thing" within. If my appropriation of Newton's ("white thing") theory holds, I wonder what the consequences will be when the postcolonial other "takes physic." Will the action of cultural erasure and racial transfiguration lead to intensified ethnic identification, sectarian struggle, and geopolitical contestation?

In part because of its engagement with theories of difference, postcoloniality as a discipline has the potential to present, in global proportions, the kind of finely honed critique of hegemonic systems that Afrocentricity as a perspective—as a therapeutic essentialism—has restricted to its own local politics. In the early 1990s I noted that the majority of scholars actively engaged in carving out the contours of postcolonial discourse were Indians. I predicted at the time that the more currency postcoloniality gained within the academy, the less this would be true. The inevitable turn away from the "authentic" Indian postcolonial to the intellectually produced postcolonialist was presaged, I argued, by a number of events around the university, including the arrival of a new generation of graduate students seeking training not in British, American, or even African American literature but in postcolonial studies.

Today there is considerable evidence that the intellectual tide has already turned, including the different first-world locations taken up in several recent publications that announce themselves as postcolonial texts. Several of these texts claim the United States, Canada, Australia, Ireland, and New Zealand as paradigmatic postcolonies, whose colonial subjects are not the native inhabitants of the land but the European settlers and their descendants. In these configurations, canonical white male authors such as Washington Irving, James Fenimore Cooper, and Herman Melville become the premier postcolonial writers. In other words, the oppositional "minority discourse" of postcoloniality is used to reaffirm the European or Anglo-American center. Such appropriations of postcolonial status may represent a form of intellectual imperialism that erases the line between colonizer and colonized. Will Indian scholars fight to hold that line, theorizing an "Indocentricity"?

As a reconstituted cultural-historical narrative, Afrocentricity serves a therapeutic function not unlike that served by other sacred texts, including the Bible and the Koran. Like the Old Testament, it is a kind of creation myth that gives a displaced people a home and a history, even as it denies the hybridity that is part of the history. My playful speculation about Indocentricity notwithstanding, I would not wish the blind spots of Afrocentricity on another discourse. What I would wish for postcoloniality—as self-congratulating as it may seem—is not the therapeutic essentialism of Afrocentricity but the strategic essentialism of an interculturally oriented African American studies. I know the faults of my own discipline too well to hold it up as a perfect model. Instead I mean only to suggest that, as a politicized discourse, African American studies falls somewhere between the hyperlocalization and nativism of Asante's Afrocentricity and the global or universal delocalization of postcoloniality. Among other things, in its insistence on a local place, African American studies implicates the same United States that postcoloniality, for the most part, lets off the imperialist hook.

I began this chapter with Du Bois's famous ruminations on double-consciousness. I want to close my own ruminations by quoting Edward Said:

No one today is purely *one* thing. Labels like Indian, or woman, or Muslim, or American are not more than starting-points, which if followed into actual experience for only a moment are quickly left behind. Imperialism consolidated the mixture of cultures and identities on a global scale. But its worst and most paradoxical gift was to allow people to believe that they were only, mainly, exclusively, white, or Black, or Western, or Oriental.[16]

Despite the decades and the racial and cultural differences that separate them, the visions of Du Bois and Said are remarkably similar. They both address how imperialism and colonization have turned the planet and its peoples upside down and inside out, so that no one is purely any one thing. But what do we do with this knowledge? To what use do we put this sense of our multiplicity, our interrelatedness, and our interdependence?

It is no accident, I suppose, that I am drawn to both Du Bois and Said—to African American discourse and to postcolonial theory. But what of Afrocentricity? Is it simply a straw man or false idol in the company of "legitimate" studies? If we could see beyond the tufts of straw and the feet of clay, I wonder what practitioners of these three discourses—African American studies, postcoloniality, and Afrocentricity—might learn from one another, and in particular what we might teach one another about the white academy that both claims and disclaims us. As we go about our intellectual business and launch our critiques, we would perhaps do well to be less suspicious of one another and more suspicious of the academy that promotes, demotes, and divides us. For if the world is out of joint, the university—traditionally a bastion of white male authority—is a perilous place to put it right.

5

The Blacker the Juice: O. J. Simpson and the Squeeze Play of Race

> When [O. J. Simpson] sprinted effortlessly through airports for Hertz cars, focus groups said that they didn't perceive him as black. He was an All-American.
>
> —"Crime and Punishment," *Mother Jones* (October 1994)

> "Look, there's O. J. Simpson and some niggers."
>
> —Simpson in 1969, quoting an overheard conversation

In 1976 Shindana Toys, the same black-owned toy company that rose out of the ashes of the Watts riots, produced the O. J. Simpson Super Pro doll. The nine-and-a-half-inch action figure came dressed in a Buffalo Bills football uniform, complete with helmet and a replica of Simpson's number-32 jersey. I doubt that anyone who purchased or played with the doll in the late 1970s could have imagined that in less than twenty years the former running back would be forced to trade his football uniform for a blue jumpsuit, the 1990s equivalent of prison stripes. Yet, from the mainstream media's coverage of what came to be known as the Simpson case, the June 1994 murders of Nicole Brown Simpson and Ronald Goldman and the subsequent trial of O. J. Simpson, one might conclude that the former All-American's spectacular fall from grace was inevitable—what black men born of the ghetto are bound to do.

Before he was arrested and tried for double homicide, Simpson reportedly believed his greatest accomplishment to be that people saw him as a man first, not as a black man. Other African Americans, including his first wife, Marguerite, might be described by whites as "some niggers,"[1] but he was forever "O.J.," pitchman, actor, all-American football legend—beloved of his country. After the murders, however, if he read the papers or watched the news or listened to his own defense (or read his own book, for that matter), what Simpson no doubt discovered was the inevitability of his own blackness. Not only was he a black man first, last, and always but, as charges of racism and the defense team's fortuitous discovery of the Fuhrman tapes cast a pall over the prosecution's case, it seemed more and more likely that Simpson's freedom—whether he would be acquitted or spend the rest of his life in prison—would depend on the very appellation from which he thought he was exempt: "nigger," "the N word."

Focusing in particular on *Time* and *Newsweek* magazines, I want to track the mainstream media's coverage of the Simpson case. Embedded in much of this coverage was a racially coded message ultimately as contemptuous of black people as the one the white high school seniors sneaked into their yearbook. I am speaking metaphorically, of course, but only somewhat. What I found in the public discourse surrounding the murders and the trial was a sometimes subtle, sometimes overt attempt to link Simpson's alleged crime to his color, to darken him, blacken him, "niggerize" him, and, especially, de-Americanize him. When he was good, he was all-American, but when he was bad, he was black. Illuminating Simpson's blackness, his "dark side," his hidden essential black self became a way of explaining the crime, which at moments seemed less that he might have murdered two people than that he had fooled millions.

If the enracing of O. J. Simpson were all there was to the media coverage, my job would be easier. But the reporting was far from monolithic or strictly divided along racial lines. Simpson himself has complimented both the talk-show host Larry King and the Associated Press correspondent Linda Deutsch for what he considers their fair reporting. In general, though, the mainstream (mostly white) media were more given to a kind of pathological coverage that not only presumed Simpson's guilt but related his crime to his black roots and his gang past, to what black men do *by nature*. If the accused walked—and many white journalists and legal experts speculated that he would—it would result from his defense team's race plays, the prosecution's bungles (especially its star witness, Los Angeles police detective Mark Fuhrman), and the black jurors' sympathetic ears, and not from his innocence.

The black press, by contrast, was generally softer on Simpson and harder on the LAPD, the prosecution, and the witnesses, especially Denise Brown. The eldest Brown sister provides a telling example of how the two wings of "Camp O.J."—the media stakeout at the courthouse—often read and reported the same events quite differently. For most of the mainstream media, Denise Brown was a sympathetic, credible witness, whose tearful testimony and striking resemblance to her slain sister tugged on the jurors' heartstrings and advanced the cause of the prosecution. This same tearful testimony was judged more malicious than material by black journalists and legal experts, as well as by many in the African American community at large, including a dismissed juror, Jeanette Harris, who characterized Brown's court appearance as "melodramatic." Both the black press and black journalists working in the mainstream media took more detailed notice of the inconsistencies in Brown's testimony: she originally denied that her sister was battered by Simpson, for example, and she, a recovering alcoholic, was often drinking heavily at the time of the events she recounted. (One black reporter dismissed both Denise Brown and prosecution witness Ron Shipp as drunks.) The discrepancy between the menacing, rejected ex-husband that Denise Brown described glowering at her sister throughout Sydney Simpson's June 12 dance recital and the congenial family man caught on videotape laughing and schmoozing with the Browns after the recital was also much remarked by African American trial watchers,[2] as were the benefits that the "n'er-do-well" Browns allegedly reaped from their seventeen-year association with their wealthy and generous inlaw. Taking their cue from Johnnie Cochran's opening statement, many black journalists were quick to repeat the claim that Simpson contributed substantially to the family's support, including setting up Nicole's father in a Hertz dealership and sending two of her sisters to college, until they dropped out. Noting her references to bar hopping, shopping sprees, and Club Med vacations, several black commentators—including NBC's Bryant Gumbel—speculated that, far from bolstering the prosecution's case, Denise Brown's court appearance may have inspired more disdain for the Simpson-supported lifestyles of the apparently idle, uneducated, unwed-mother Brown sisters than sympathy for the murder victim.[3]

Curiously, though, even some of the pro-defendant coverage focused more on the system's guilt than on Simpson's innocence. Ishmael Reed, one of six prominent African Americans invited to comment on the case in the pages of *Ebony,* spoke the words on the lips of millions: "Thousands of Black citizens are convicted by the media, in most cases without even having been charged with a crime. Since the media are 50 years behind the South in the efforts to integrate, these Blacks are convicted by the new all-White jury: journalists, media critics, talk show hosts, psychologists, TV columnists, and assorted quacks."[4] Like most of the other commentators, Reed indicted the white media and the white judicial system, but stopped short of affirming Simpson's innocence. Similar sentiments were expressed by Dennis Schatzman, a black journalist covering the trial for the *Los Angeles Sentinel,* an African American weekly. When the prosecution finally rested after twenty-four weeks of testimony,

Schatzman called their case a six-million-dollar boondoggle. "The easiest person in the world to convict is a black man," he told the *New Yorker*. "We're already guilty in the minds of the public. You don't even need evidence. What happened to O.J. has happened to a lot of black people. This is the case for people to see it."[5]

Schatzman's comments, however potent and historically resonant, are more than a little ironic, since he himself had publicly admitted stalking, shooting, and quite possibly killing a man who shot him in 1990. Schatzman was never charged with the crime, and since he refused to name his victim, he evidently felt he was beyond the reach of the law. Seemingly unremorseful about either crime or punishment, he told the host of CBS's *American Journal*, "vengeance is mine, sayeth the Lord—and Dennis Schatzman."[6] Confession is good for the soul, they say, and Schatzman does have terminal cancer, but admitting to prior drug use and possible homicide in the midst of covering the murder trial of a black man he insisted was framed by a system that criminalizes all black men didn't do much for an otherwise cogent argument.

It was widely reported in 1995 that approximately one third of the young black male population in the United States was negatively involved with the criminal justice system: under arrest, on or awaiting trial, in prison, or on parole. Moreover, half of those young black men not incarcerated or in custody were said to be unemployed. Given these sobering statistics, it is more than a little strange that the argument about the color biases of the law was made so vociferously on behalf of Simpson, who by virtue of his fame and fortune was far better able to buy justice—or at least expert legal counsel and investigative services—than the typical black male defendant. Yet multitudes rallied to Simpson's support, including family, friends, and hordes of fans who rimmed the highway cheering "Go, O.J., Go!" during the infamous June 17 Bronco chase and who came to the courthouse throughout the trial carrying signs with messages such as GUILTY OR NOT WE LOVE U OJ. Ultimately more useful than the cheers of fans, however, were the pleas of black leaders, including Jesse Jackson, who came forward in the summer of 1994 to persuade District Attorney Gil Garcetti not to seek the death penalty for Simpson, arguing that death rows in prisons across the country are disproportionately populated by black men. This is sadly and horribly true, but the argument has been much less effective outside the glare of television cameras.

Although the press, like the public, generally has been tough on crime and uncaring about criminals, some of the mainstream coverage of the Simpson case had a surprisingly pro-defendant quality, most often at the expense of the victims, who were cast by implication in the role of provocateurs. Again, it was not that "O.J."—as the press insisted on calling him—was presumed innocent but that his crime of passion was somehow justified by the philandering of a flighty, ungrateful wife (the "ex" was often omitted), who let her handsome, twenty-five-year-old "friend" Ron Goldman drive the white Ferrari that Simpson's money paid for and who went so far as to have a (post-divorce) affair with her husband's good friend Marcus Allen. A front-page photo in the *National Enquirer* of Nicole Simpson with her arms around two white men, one of whom has his hands on her breasts, helped to confirm Simpson in the role of cuckolded husband.[7] Such photos and the revelation that (according to what we hear him shouting in the background on a 911 tape) he observed his ex-wife and her lover having oral sex on her living room couch, while the children slept upstairs, were enough to get Simpson a sympathetic nod from the ultraconservative talk-show host Rush Limbaugh. Limbaugh played the tape for his listeners, pointing out that Simpson only threatened his ex-wife, which is not a crime.

Even some of her own friends likened Nicole Simpson to a Barbie doll, not a particularly flattering comparison in my estimation. Other media coverage, such as *Sports Illustrated*'s June 27 cover story, peppered their reportage with quotations from anonymous friends and associates who insisted that Nicole "was no young innocent"; she knew what buttons to push. "When this all comes out, you'll see that she wasn't little Miss Suzy Home-maker," one member of their circle, a football player, is quoted as saying. "She had an alcohol problem. She'd get drunk and say and do things you normally wouldn't do . . . She knew how to set him off."[8] The same article quotes from the Simpsons' divorce papers, detailing the extravagant life the couple had lived together, and goes on to speculate that the $24,000 a month that an aging and less marketable Simpson was ordered to pay in alimony and child support—along with Nicole's "willful, spirited" ways—may have helped to drive O.J. to commit homicide.

But I am getting ahead of the coverage I want to uncover. Let me say for the moment that, though there were different kinds of attention given the case, I am particularly interested in what I see as the dominant mode of the reporting. From the first repeatedly reproduced image of the not-yet-accused Simpson in handcuffs on June 13, 1994, to parting shots of the acquitted Simpson on October 3, 1995, the camera lens was anything but neutral, innocent, or objective in its gaze. It is interesting to note, for instance, that as the court clerk read the verdict, the camera zoomed in not on the clerk, whose disembodied voice intoned "not guilty," but on the full-screen face of the defendant, thus subjecting that face to endless readings. Was it a smile of relief or a sneer of defiance that the defendant wore at the instant of his acquittal? Mediated through the hyperreality of television, Simpson's facial expression and body language became for many viewers additional evidence of his guilt.

Given the technological fishbowl in which we live, it is, as John Fiske and other media specialists have argued, impossible to distinguish between real events and their media representation.[9] In identifying the coverage of the Simpson case as racially coded, I am not suggesting that somewhere out there was a pure, unadulterated "real" event that the fourth estate, with malice aforethought, colorized and misrepresented. Nor is my critique meant to imply that we, the people, are all naive readers, blindly led down a newsprint path by an all-powerful press. But whatever we know or think we know about the Simpson case, we know through the prism of the press, and it would be a mistake to underestimate the media's ability not simply to inform the public but to shape its opinion. What needs to be addressed, then, is the ideological work of both the news and the entertainment media—and how race and capital can blur the line between the two. What needs to be examined is the extent to which the media function as what the Marxist philosopher Louis Althusser called "ideological state apparatuses," institutions that reinforce the views of dominant culture and capital and, in so doing, serve the interests of the State.

Yet sometimes the workings of the press run counter to reigning interests: the subversive investigative reporting of Carl Bernstein and Bob Woodward in the *Washington Post,* for example, which helped to unseat Nixon in 1974. In the case of *The People v. O. J. Simpson,* however, the media collaborated with the State of California in the presumption not of innocence, as the law allows, but of guilt. Moreover, this collective production of guilt was racially nuanced. Cast in most media circles as the slyest black trickster of all time, Brer Simpson was perhaps most often written of as a black beast who donned whiteface and duped the nation into granting him its most precious prize: not the Heisman trophy, not fame, wealth, and success, not even the white wife, but the title All-American. But whatever his crime, duping or double murder, and however un-American his activities, Simpson was first and foremost good copy, a bestseller—not just a media happening but an entrepreneurial event as well.

Whatever others have made of it, no single recent event more dramatically illustrates the meaning and the marketability of race than the tragedy called "the crime of the century" and "the trial of the century."[10] Hero or murderer, innocent or guilty, O. J. Simpson quickly became a cash crop that made fortunes for many, even as millions of taxpayers' dollars were eaten away by court and trial costs. T-shirts, trading cards, tell-all books, tabloid talk shows, TV movies, and a battery of talking heads (legal experts paid as much as $4000 a day for their commentary) all became part of a new industry that one network executive described as "gorging on the buffet" of O. J. Simpson.[11]

Murder and mayhem among the rich and famous have always played well with the masses. The 1935 trial of Bruno Hauptmann for the murder of the Lindbergh baby created such a media circus and caused such public hysteria that cameras were banned from the courtroom for the next forty-two years. But with the Simpson case, race also helped to turn a tragedy into a moneymaking bonanza. Indeed, many people—especially African Americans—speculated that had the victims been Simpson's black ex-wife and a black male friend, there would have been far less media attention and public fascination. Others suggested with equal cynicism that if all the players were white—victims, accused, attorneys, judge, and jury—if, heaven forbid, Frank Gifford were accused of murdering Regis and Kathie Lee—the event would not have had the carnival air that permeated the Simpson trial.[12]

In reality, though, the historically volatile racial dynamics of this particular case—white female and male victims and a black male celebrity assailant—gave cinemascopic dimension to a horror story, the movie version of which might be titled *The Rebirth of a Nation*, in dubious tribute to D. W. Griffith's 1915 film. Based on the anti-Reconstruction tracts of Thomas Dixon, Griffith's *Birth of a Nation* portrays freed black men (white actors in blackface) lusting murderously after innocent white women. The need to protect white womanhood from the sexual threat posed by black men serves as the rationale for the rise of the Ku Klux Klan in Dixon's novels *The Leopard's Spots: A Romance of the White Man's Burden* (1902) and *The Clansman: A Historical Romance of the Ku Klux Klan* (1905) and in Griffith's film, for which Dixon wrote the screenplay. In fiction and film, the excessive sexual appetites that black men supposedly have for white women is depicted as a desire to marry them.[13] In real life, black men have been lynched because someone said they looked at, spoke to, or thought about a white woman. Here in the form of O. J. Simpson was a black man who had bedded, wedded, and maybe murdered a beautiful, blond homecoming princess, killing as well her gallant (if accidental) white male champion. The media and the masses could do no less than go wild.

The pretrial release of highly inflammatory 911 tapes helped to transform Simpson from an innocuous, some say raceless, American icon into the archetypal, sexually threatening black male beast about whom Dixon and Griffith had long ago warned white America. The instantaneous publication of *Nicole Brown Simpson: The Private Diary of a Life Interrupted* (1994)—Faye Resnick's sleazy tableau of domestic violence, drug abuse, lesbian love, and jungle-fever fatal attraction—helped to ensure Simpson's metamorphosis from man to monster.[14] Hitting or, rather, drawing our attention below the belt, Resnick's book not only pronounced Simpson guilty of murder, it also reconfirmed all of the stereotypes about black male criminality, sexual prowess, and carnal deviance. Within its pages, the affable prince charming the world saw on the screen is exposed as a hard-drinking, drug-doing, wife-beating womanizer—morbidly jealous, obsessed with sex and with his ex-wife.

But the racialization and sensationalization of the drama claimed other characters as well. The defense team's ultimately successful attempt to expose Mark Fuhrman as a racist white cop with a history of using the N word and a special animus against interracial coupling fed the racial frenzy. If Simpson was essentially black, Fuhrman, his fellow cop conspirators, and the entire judicial system were quintessentially white. Could justice be blind, deaf, and dumb to such color codes? Could a black man get a fair trial in white America? Or was this case destined to become the "high-tech lynching" that Clarence Thomas invoked during his confirmation hearings, playing to his advantage the race card he otherwise denied was in the deck?

Reshuffling a Marked Deck

In August 1994, defense attorney Robert Shapiro insisted that "race is not and will not be an issue" in the Simpson case. For those who believe that race is always an issue in a color-conscious, racially stratified society such as ours, the assertion rang with such naiveté that it could only have been made by someone whose white privilege had shielded him from the deep structures and long reaches of racism in America.[15] For Johnnie Cochran, the eminent black attorney who joined Simpson's team of white lawyers shortly before Shapiro's assertion, race was not only an issue; it was *the* issue.[16] "I think race plays a part of everything in America, let alone this trial," he later told two *Newsweek* correspondents.[17] Cochran soon began to mount a defense that painted Simpson as yet another black male victim of a racially motivated police conspiracy—a strategy that many feel contributed to acquittal but that led a disgruntled Shapiro to declare on national television: "Not only did we play the race card, we dealt it from the bottom of the deck."[18]

Many trial observers have argued, as Cochran himself has insisted, that the complexities of racism cannot be reduced to a deck of playing cards. But like any good lawyer, Cochran is adept at talking out of both sides of his month; like any good poker player, he knows when to hold. Race may be more than a playing card, but Cochran knew from the start what the defense had in its hand. Even before he officially joined the dream team, he had concluded that race—as he later said of the Fuhrman tapes—was a bombshell that the defense would likely "exploit" (his word). It should not have come as any surprise, then, that the race-card metaphor stuck, as race, in the words of *Newsweek*, increasingly permeated the trial, "from the strategies tried, to the players brought on stage, to the evidence itself."[19]

Indeed, in jury selection, in conspiracy theories, in the repeated polling of black and white audiences, the so-called race card was played so often that both the celebrity and the race of the accused threatened to eclipse the tragic deaths of the victims. But it wasn't only the defense that anteed up. In what many read as a transparent race play of its own, the prosecution added a black deputy district attorney, Christopher Darden, to its all-white team, after the seating of a predominantly African American jury. This move placed Darden on the wrong side of the racial divide, as it were, and made him look like the prosecution's Uncle Tom. Despite his own somewhat Johnnie-come-lately addition to what had been an all-white defense team, Cochran was not above baiting his brother lawyer about his token status.[20] On more than one occasion (the battle over whether the word "nigger" could be spoken in front of the jury, for example), Cochran implicitly questioned Darden's racial authenticity and allegiance.

Journalists and talking-head lawyers played their own games of racial roulette, egged on by endless polls—all supposedly showing that the nation was deeply divided along racial lines on the issue of Simpson's guilt or innocence. (I say "supposedly" both because no one polled me or anyone I know and because such polls must always be inflected by variables of class, gender, education, age, location, and religion.) Although percentages fluctuated throughout the trial, the reported polarity remained constant: a majority of white Americans—anywhere from 60 to 80 percent—believed Simpson guilty, and a majority of black Americans judged him innocent. The polls and the predominantly black jury led many reporters and legal analysts to conclude that the prosecution faced a nearly impossible task in trying to win a conviction. In article after article and talk show after talk show, race—more so than class or celebrity or even the "mountain of evidence"—was cast as the trump card. Black jurors, experts argued, might not necessarily buy defense theories about Colombian druglords and planted evidence, but their own racial experience was likely to make them more inclined toward reasonable doubt, more predisposed to see Simpson as another black victim of the white judicial system.

Yet as potent as the race question became, the first two weeks following the murders were curiously free of spoken or written references to race. The mainstream media focused instead on wife battering, whose immediate relevance and dire consequences served to justify all the obsessive attention to the case.

John Fiske has even suggested that the media and the nation experienced a kind of "confessional relief" at being able to use Nicole Simpson's death to shed light on the hidden crime of domestic violence. He also noted that, in an uncharacteristically self-critical gesture, the media treated their own role in covering up Simpson's history of spousal abuse "as symptomatic of the more general cover-up by which America refuses to recognize one of its most common crimes."[21]

But racism is also one of America's most enduring crimes, and it too has been covered up or refused public forum. In the fracturing of issues and identities so common in public discourse, the mainstream media's early gendering of the crime diverted attention from the racial dimensions of the case, even as it used a black man and racially coded language—the killings were savage, brutal, bestial, barbaric, dark, demonic—to dramatize and color yet another major national issue. Even where the words "black" and "African American" remained unspoken, wife beating took on a decidedly dark cast, as Simpson became the metonymic signifier for all male violence. In this way, the mainstream media's representation of Nicole Simpson as the archetypal battered wife played directly into age-old anxieties about black male brutality and criminality—in effect justifying those anxieties while "race" remained largely unspoken.[22]

On one television broadcast just days after the murders, the sportscaster Dick Schaaf—one of few media personalities to mention race at all—tried in vain to get his fellow white ESPN panelists to agree that Simpson rose above race. "Don't you think O.J. transcended race like a Bill Cosby or a Sidney Poitier?" Schaaf asked at least three times, but no one would bite. It was as if he had never spoken. Schaaf's question is certainly a loaded one, both because it suggests the possibility that some blacks can rise above race—which means become "white like us"—and because it associates that possibility with the entertainment world, with those who are perceived, professionally speaking, as "acting white." Both Poitier and Cosby have been perennially good guys, often playing the role of what the black scholar Anthony Appiah calls the "saint"—"the black man who is too good to be true," whose superior virtue and nonthreatening goodness make him acceptable to white society.[23] Schaaf seemed to be suggesting that Simpson's brilliant football career, good-guy public persona, and "ingratiating personal style"[24] had entitled him, too, to honorary whiteness. But however anxious Schaaf was to talk that talk, no one else on the panel was willing to come within a hundred yards of this particular N zone.

With a picture worth more than a thousand chants of "Go, O.J., Go," *Time* magazine blew the lid off the racial powder keg that the media had been tiptoeing around. When the June 27 issues of *Time* and *Newsweek* hit the stands with markedly different versions of the same Simpson mugshot on their covers, not only was the ace of spades out of the deck but the sinister black cat was out of the bag. *Newsweek* published the mugshot photo more or less as is, but *Time* darkened and blurred the image of O. J. Simpson. The alterations made the subject look more sinister, more guilty—more like "some kind of animal," according to Benjamin Chavis, then executive director of the NAACP. In the words of one white media critic, the *Time* cover effectively sent Simpson "back to the ghetto."[25]

As many people commenting on the controversial cover pointed out (including *Time*'s managing editor in a note to readers published the following week), it is itself racist to read darker or blacker as more sinister. Yet this is precisely the color signification on which the western world has turned since time immemorial. *Time* may claim it intended "no racial implication" or "imputation of guilt," but white/black, good/evil imagery is so *natural*, so potent, and so thoroughly internalized in our society that it needs neither intention nor interpretation. The *Time* cover pronounced in graphic terms the unspoken, unwritten, perpetually present racial narrative.

This narrative is also enunciated by the words emblazoned across Simpson's chest, just above his prison number in bold, blood-red print: "An American Tragedy."[26] *Time*'s managing editor called the headline "simple" and "nonjudgmental." I would argue, however, that far from being either neutral or innocuous, the words "An American Tragedy" collaborate with the darkened mugshot in complex, compelling, and decidedly colored and gendered ways. Precisely what is the tragedy to which the headline alludes: the slaying of two people, neither of whose picture appears on the cover; a hero's collision with "his dark side";[27] or America's collision with its own grief and disbelief? Even government officials were confused about what the tragedy was and who the victims were. Richard Halverson, the chaplain for the U.S. Senate, called upon the chamber to join him in praying for O. J. Simpson and for the nation traumatized by the fall of a great hero. Neither Nicole Simpson nor Ron Goldman was mentioned.

Noting the absence of the murder victims' pictures on *Time*'s "American Tragedy" cover, Wendy Kozol insists that we must ask not only for whom is this a tragedy but also "why is this specifically an 'American' tragedy? What is the linkage between the personal and national in this murder? And why is race an integral factor in this story of domesticity gone awry?"[28] Kozol answers her own questions by suggesting that these murders upset the domestic ideals central to the American family romance. To the extent that O. J. Simpson functioned iconographically as the "'nonblack' hero" who embodied "the American dream of individual success," his fall from grace "upsets national ideologies of equality and opportunity." Like the darkened mugshot and the many mini-biographies exposing Simpson's childhood poverty, broken home, and brushes with the law, the headline works to "articulate his difference and explain his fall."

Kozol's reading seems on the mark, but I think we can push it a few steps farther. First, the fact that images of Nicole Simpson and Ronald Goldman are missing from the cover and the coverage more generally suggests just how much the fall of black celebrity O. J. Simpson is the actual American tragedy, the real story, the better copy. Except in those rare moments when the media became self-conscious about their own inattention to the two victims,[29] Goldman was never much more than an "also-killed" footnote in the reporting of the case. Similarly, Nicole Brown Simpson's function was also symbolic. Even as her murder drew national attention to the crime of domestic violence, the victim herself was curiously written out of her own story. *Time* followed up its "American Tragedy" issue with an eight-page cover story on domestic abuse, published the next week. Nicole Brown Simpson was neither on the cover nor in the story.[30] Her absence may be explained by the extent to which her not-so-nice-girl image upsets the *Birth of a Nation* narrative. Americans like the female victims of black male brutality to be pure (or at least discreet), and Nicole Simpson had already made the mistake of sleeping with the enemy and having his brown babies. Some of the coverage came close to implying that she had invited her own murder, and even her sister cast doubts on her status as a battered wife. Although Denise Brown has since made a career of crusading against the domestic violence of which she now insists her sister was a victim, at first she vehemently denied that Nicole was beaten. "She was not a battered woman," Brown told the *New York Times* in a telephone interview ten days after the murders. "She was a very strong-willed person. If she was beaten up, she wouldn't have stayed with him. That wasn't her. Everybody knows about 1989. Does anybody know about any other times?"[31] Six months later, Denise Brown, now head of the Nicole Brown Simpson Charitable Foundation for Battered Women, testified that there were indeed other times she herself had witnessed, that she had in fact taken pictures of her sister's bruised body. Even given that battered women often hide the fact of their abuse from their families and friends, the Browns' blissful ignorance has been hard for some to fathom and may have cost Nicole Simpson much more than just a magazine cover story.

There is a second point I want to make about the caption *Time* put on its June 27 cover. Whether intended to or not, "An

American Tragedy" evokes Theodore Dreiser's novel of 1925. Based on an actual murder trial in Herkimer County, New York, Dreiser's *An American Tragedy* chronicles the life and crime of Clyde Griffiths, a young white man who, much like the young O. J. Simpson, is determined to escape the poverty and pathology of his childhood to claim the wealth, women, and success that are the seductive promise of the white male American dream. But the dream explodes in Griffiths's face, and he is tried, convicted, and electrocuted for drowning the pregnant girlfriend who stood in his way. The tragedy that drives Dreiser's novel is particularly American, we are made to understand, because the protagonist is at once the product and the victim of a corrupt, materialistic society that tempts the poor with the same riches it withholds from them.

Linked by title and crime to Dreiser's antihero, the would-be colorless, racially transcendent Simpson is represented in *Time* (and elsewhere in the press) as a product not simply of a corrupt white society but of his own inescapable black American past. He is not a symbol of the American dream—the self-made man who pulled himself up by his jockstrap—but the walking manifestation of the nation's worst nightmare. And the drama is not simply *Guess Who's Coming to Dinner?* (He's black, *but* he's a doctor) but look who's buying your house: Willie Horton with a smile and a bank account and courting your daughter. Darkening Simpson—enracing him graphically—metaphorically returned him to his proper place and set the stage for the psychosocial exposés that followed in the hundreds of stories devoted to the case. In this sense, the altered-mugshot cover is a masterpiece of racial signification.

Wahneema Lubiano has suggested that some pictures serve as cover stories in and of themselves, both masking and revealing political power. "Like the 'covers' of secret agents," she writes, "cover stories are faces for other texts, different texts. They are pretexts that obscure context, fade out subtexts."[32] Taken together, *Time*'s "American Tragedy" headline and the photo mask and reveal in this way. But though much has been made of *Time*'s graphic blunder, less has been said about the accompanying article, whose racially charged metaphors paint an equally dark portrait of the O. J. Simpson nobody knew.

In a telling bit of armchair psychoanalysis, the cover story declares: "In crisis, people condense into their essential selves. O.J. was, essentially, a very great runner." The writer then goes on to express disdain for the Los Angeles police department and the district attorney's office, which "let the most famous double-murder suspect in history slip away under their noses" simply because they "never thought he would run." Running, after all, was part of Simpson's essential self, his basic nature. It was how "a bow-legged kid with rickets had escaped the slums where he was born . . . outrunning his obstacles, finding daylight where there wasn't any."[33]

So written, the San Francisco projects in which Simpson grew up become a kind of dark continent—a tangle of pathology (Simpson after all is the product of a single-parent, female-headed household)—suffused with obstacles and deprived of daylight. Like the instantly infamous "American Tragedy" cover, the opening paragraphs of *Time*'s story use racially loaded imagery to shed light on Simpson's darker self. The essential Simpson, the metaphors seem to say, was not just a runner but a restless native, who by the luck of his legs managed to run away from the concrete jungle that was his natural habitat.

That natural habitat was revisited throughout the trial, perhaps most notably in the testimony of defense witness Robert Huizenga, the internist who, at the request of Shapiro, examined Simpson shortly after the murders. Called to the witness stand on July 14, 1995, Dr. Huizenga offered a poetic reading of the defendant's physical condition: Simpson may look like Tarzan, the doctor declared, but he walks like Tarzan's grandfather. Given all the physically fit specimens he might have referred to—Superman, Rambo, Rocky, Hulk Hogan, or even Mr. T—it is significant that Huizenga reached back into the jungle and, without missing a beat, likened Simpson to Tarzan the ape man.

Huizenga's simile was widely quoted by the mainstream media: *Rivera Live* called its July 14 show "Tarzan's Grandfather," and *Newsweek* cited Huizenga as a good witness who "talked in sound bites" that could be "easily digested by jurors."[34] As near as I can tell, though, the racism implicit in the doctor's jungle imagery went unremarked in the popular press. Huizenga was clearly a well-intentioned, pro-Simpson witness. That such a witness could so unselfconsciously make such a slip—and get away with it—suggests just how deeply embedded in American culture such metaphors and codes are.

Tarzan Meets Barbie

On the football field, Tarzan the running back caught the ball and sprinted toward the goal line. On the larger playing field of life, he grasped not only the proverbial brass ring but one of the principal signifiers of the American dream: a white woman. As *Newsweek* crassly put it, quoting "a close friend" of Nicole Simpson, this charmed and charming black man not only got to marry a "*drop-dead* gorgeous" white woman, "who looked like a Barbie doll," but he also got her to "wait on him hand and foot and have his children."[35] (The emphasis here is mine since, in its haste to score a point about Simpson and what some have called the Othello Syndrome, *Newsweek* wrote right past the gauche, macabre irony of the friend's unfortunate metaphor.) Inscribed in this and similar narratives is the judgment that Simpson gained access to the white kingdom, including the white trophy wife, "by disguising his inner life"—something he first learned to do in the Potrero Hill housing project. To prove their point, several articles quoted Simpson himself: "The ghetto," he wrote in his autobiography in 1970, made "you want to hide your real identity—from cops, from teachers, and even from yourself. And it forces you to build up false images."[36]

False images, we are meant to understand, become false idols. But the essential self—like murder—will out. According to the same *Newsweek* cover story, as early as 1968 his wife

Marguerite described Simpson in "an unguarded interview" as "a beast," who in high school had not allowed other boys to talk to her. "He, however, was free to roam," as beasts do. The article then shares with us an in-flight episode that "Marguerite later recalled," in which Simpson encouraged the advances of an infatuated flight attendant by telling her that the woman seated next to him (Marguerite) was his sister, not his wife. "I have been shoved out of the way, pushed and stepped on by more than one beautiful woman," the magazine quotes Marguerite Simpson as saying.

In a clever move *Newsweek* managed not only to put the first Mrs. O. J. Simpson on the stand in the court of public opinion, but also to take the word "beast" right out of her mouth—out of its sixties context—transport it across a quarter of a century, and use it to punctuate its own contemporary narrative. Simpson, we learn from the best of all possible witnesses—his high school sweetheart and first wife—was always a beast with a Me-Tarzan-You-Jane approach to gender relations. Football may have taken the poor black kid out of the ghetto, but ultimately not even fame, fortune, gentlemanly golf games with presidents,[37] elocution lessons, and a white wife could take the ghetto beast out of the black man. In times of crisis, not only would he condense into his essential black self, but he would also slip into "a black accent, a lower-class accent, that was not an educated way to speak."[38]

Of this tendency to revert to type, *Time* magazine's "American Tragedy" story observes: "[Simpson] did not so much change, from the days of his raw, painful childhood, as add layers, coats of polish that only occasionally peeled." The article then goes on to relate an incident in which Simpson slipped back into "his first language, the street-corner argot of his gang years," while filming a television commercial in Oakland. Furious with himself, he was heard to remark: "That's what happens when I spend too much time with my boys . . . I forget how to talk white."[39] Having presented us with Simpson "showing his nigger," as the saying goes, and then slipping back into whiteface, the *Time* article concludes that Simpson wasn't a phony; he was just a man who had come a long way from his roots. Of course the point is to show us that he *was* a phony, that he pretended to be something he was not, that he was a black man playing at being white. *Newsweek*'s cover story doesn't apologize for its personal revelations. It cites as evidence of Simpson's peelable polish the notorious tape of his ex-wife's call to police headquarters on October 25, 1993: "On the tape, Simpson's careful diction is gone," the article informs us. "He taunts Nicole for calling the '*po*-lice' and screams profanities at her." The writers take pains to make it clear that in such jealous rages Simpson, who "practiced his diction to sound more 'white' as a corporate spokesman," was unable to control either his passions or his pronunciation. Like straightened hair in a rainstorm, he went back to snap, so to speak, and, as black folks are wont to do, put the accent on the wrong syl-lá-ble. "A double life can become too much to bear," *Newsweek* psychologized. "It is amazing . . . how long Simpson kept up the facade."[40]

Wife beating and double homicide notwithstanding, the crimes against society preoccupying these and scores of other double-life cover stories were alternately Simpson's white pretensions and his black retentions. The question of whether people "sound like their race" did come up at one point during the trial,[41] but this courtroom exchange occurred more than a year after these stories about Simpson's elocution lessons, his attempts to talk white, his lusting after white women, and his unquenchable thirst for sex. *Newsweek* was so anxious to make its point about his penchant for white women that it published a completely uncontextualized color photograph of a grinning Simpson surrounded by four young white women, each of whom is wearing a "Hawaiian Tropic" banner and holding a glass. The accompanying caption reads: "PARTY GUY / The pitchman was also a high-liver who, sources said, took drugs and joined in random sex."[42]

Taken together, the photo and the caption imply that there's a whole lotta somethin' goin' on—or about to be. But if I overread, I'm not alone. The publication of the photo with only that suggestive caption drew an angry response from at least one of the young women pictured, who resented the implication that she was part of Simpson's harem. According to her, she and the other women pictured are models, who were not partying with Simpson but simply posing for a publicity shot at the behest of Hawaiian Tropic, the suntan-oil manufacturer that hired them.

Of the many photographs in this eight-page special report, at least one other requires comment: a full-page color shot of Simpson gazing off into the distance, at what we don't know. In the bottom right-hand corner of the same page is a second photograph, a tiny snapshot of a black man—presumably Simpson, although only the pearly white teeth of a wide grin are clearly visible. The man is dressed all in white and seated casually on a bench or box. In front of him, with her back toward him, a white woman in a skimpy bikini is bending over from the waist, her legs spread apart in an inverted V as if she were doing toe-touching exercises. She has very pale skin, a thin, Barbie-doll body, and massive red hair. This photo, too, has no context, but a caption under it reads: "DUTY AND OBSESSION / He was a perfectionist who doggedly worked to fit into the white world—affable, genial, and unthreatening. But Nicole left him. And his black friends scorned him for lusting after only white women." What is remarkable about these two photos—the full-page portrait of the gazing Simpson and the superimposed snapshot of the grinning Simpson—is the extent to which they position the accused murderer as a voyeur, the object of whose gaze is the white woman. The photos, especially the snapshot, repeat the many scenes in *Birth of a Nation* in which black men lurk in the background, leering at and lusting after unsuspecting white women. Both picture and caption suggest that the grinning Simpson has similar lusts, while his white clothes and the black border around the snapshot and caption (printed in white ink) affirm that this is a black and white drama. The affable Simpson may be dressed in the white clothing of a lamb, but the bold type on the facing page tells us "Day & Night / He lived two lives."

Talking Texts, Speaking Race

These light/dark cover stories, by no means limited to *Time* and *Newsweek,* speak their coded racial narratives all the more profoundly when they are considered in the context of general news coverage. In the mainstream media, certain tropes—jungle motifs, for example—and a whole spectrum of color metaphors seem to be specially reserved for the dark crimes of dark people. *Newsweek*'s treatment of the accused Oklahoma City bomber, Timothy McVeigh, is a case in point.

On July 3, 1995, the cover of *Newsweek* featured a large color portrait of a wistful, even angelic, blond, blue-eyed McVeigh, looking for all the world like, in the words of his attorney, "the boy next door, a boy wonder."[43] McVeigh, who when the photo was taken stood accused of killing 168 men, women, and children, had been dubbed the most hated man in America. Nevertheless *Newsweek* chose for its cover not a mugshot but a glossy Hollywood glamor shot. The photo is complemented by a cover story and a jailhouse interview telling us that McVeigh, who grew up among Boy Scouts in a small town in upstate New York, appeared "good humored and self-aware. Normal." Although the coauthors of the first article do note that normality is the image McVeigh wants to project, there is no attempt to blacken the cherub; there are no references to a "dark side," a "double life," a sinister "essential self," or even a hidden agenda. Instead, both the story and the interview imply that with McVeigh what you see is what you get: normal, the boy next door—someone who doesn't "*seem* like a baby killer."[44] And what does a baby killer—or any killer—seem or look like? We know from the easy nationwide acceptance of the fabrications of white killers such as Susan Smith and Charles Stuart, both of whom blamed their own hideous homicides on mythical black assailants, that most

Americans more readily visualize a black man in the role of murderer than a white woman or man.[45]

Newsweek's portrayal of McVeigh as "a wistful, ingenuous youth" drew angry responses from readers, who accused the magazine of, in the words of one letter writer, "serving up a 'love-shoot' that all but transformed a creep into 'America's newest altar boy.'" One protester went so far as to demand an apology from the magazine: "If you had captioned the photo 'The Innocent Face of Evil,' I might have understood. But as it is, you owe an apology to the American people for this affront to our sensibilities."[46] McVeigh is of course entitled to the presumption of innocence, but the friendly soldier-to-soldier treatment he received within the pages of *Newsweek* is stunning, particularly in comparison to the handling of Simpson or, as another angry letter writer pointed out, the treatment given the alleged masterminds of the World Trade Center bombing. But, then, the media in general seemed far more interested in the Oklahoma tragedy when the perpetrators were assumed to be Arab or other dark-skinned terrorists—sand niggers—from "over there," rather than some of America's own angry white sons. Even before McVeigh was in handcuffs, it was back to "O.J." as usual.

Most of the stories and photographs that *Time* and *Newsweek* used to document the Simpson case during the fifteen months I followed their coverage seem to me more prurient than probative, more inflammatory than informative. As such, they are more in keeping with the checkbook journalism of the *National Enquirer* and *Star* magazine (which I also followed) than with the responsible reporting one expects from *Time* and *Newsweek*.[47] By the magazines' own, I think, inadvertent admission, the tone and texture of their coverage of the Simpson case seem to have been shaped less by a duty to inform the public than by a need to compete with the "wide-open" checkbooks of the tabloids. In its October 9, 1995, issue *Newsweek* applauded itself for its ability to compete "amid the ravenous media pack" that descended on the Simpson trial. The magazine seemed particularly proud of its many firsts, which it itemized for its readers:

> *Newsweek* was the first publication to report that the L.A. district attorney would not seek the death penalty for Simpson. We revealed that the defense's "mystery envelope" contained a knife, and that serious strains had emerged between Simpson attorneys Robert Shapiro and F. Lee Bailey. Six weeks after O.J.'s arrest, we reported that the defense's strategy would be to impugn the credibility of the LAPD and former detective Mark Fuhrman in particular. And we remained ahead on the Fuhrman story, reporting that he betrayed signs of racism during a secret mock examination, a disclosure that became a major issue in the trial. Even after the case went to the jury last week, *Newsweek* got the first in-depth print interview with Simpson lawyer Johnnie Cochran.[48]

The article ends by informing us of the awards *Newsweek* won in 1994 (including one for its "Trail of Blood" cover story), noting that its own "'dream team' kept pace in 1995, cutting through the hype and sleaze to apply an exceptional mixture of aggressive reporting and thoughtful analysis to a story that, like it or not, has become a national obsession."

Not to be outdone, *Time* followed suit the next week with a presidential message "To Our Readers," in which it congratulated itself for its success in nobly pursuing the story "the old-fashioned way: by getting to the right sources," even as TV and tabloid reporters offered tens of thousands of dollars for exclusives. "*Time,* like most serious news publications, does not pay for interviews," the article explained. Still the magazine was able to get "the cops to open up despite an L.A.P.D. gag order" and to land key interviews with Johnnie Cochran and the Goldman family. If *Newsweek* cut through the hype and sleaze, *Time,* according to its own press, "penetrate[d] the haze" of the "smoke-filled rooms" where the real action was.[49]

Far from cutting through or rising above the sleaze, hype, and haze, *Time* and *Newsweek* seemed to wallow in the slime with the best—or worst—of them. It was *Newsweek,* not *Star* or the *Enquirer,* that published a tacky weekly "Trial Scorecard" in which it awarded from one to five gavels to the defense, the prosecution, and the judge, as if the trial were indeed just another football game. And, though a reporter's job is certainly to get the story by almost any means necessary, I'm not sure that getting officers of the law to break a gag order is a strategy to boast about.

More important, these self-congratulatory accounts of who scooped whom—of how *Newsweek* held it own "amid the ravenous media pack," of how *Time* got the goods without paying big bucks like the tabloids—speak volumes about the collusion between media culture and capitalism. It is not just a matter of public information, of "the facts, ma'am, just the facts," or of simply reporting all the news that's fit to print. The production of news, like other modes of production, is profit-driven. In our postmodern, capitalistic society, the free market mandates prurience rather than probity, entertainment more than enlightenment. Figured not only as the crime but also as the racial/sexual high-society spectacle of the century, the Simpson scandal is good news precisely because it is good business. And the blacker the Juice, the bigger the sales.

But to try to put a somewhat more positive spin on what I have alleged is both the prurience and the racism of these texts, the junk journalism in which the "serious" press indulged in its coverage of the Simpson case was in some measure an almost desperate attempt to explain the inexplicable. The same *Time* cover story that begins with the darkened mugshot and an analysis of Simpson's essential black self also speaks movingly of a grief-stricken nation's frenzied quest for answers in the wake of the murders of two innocent people and the arrest of a national icon: "Pundits trotted out Shakespeare for references," the article informs us; "talk-radio hosts searched for Larger Meanings . . . But by the end of the week, with the last astounding twists of the case, it seemed that there were no larger meanings—just a howling, monstrous tragedy," with millions of fans "mourning not only two victims they had never known, but the hero they thought they did."[50]

This is an eloquent account of the mourning after. But the trouble is that time and time again the search for cause—the struggle to understand the dark side of the fallen hero—is located in Simpson's racial difference, in the true-blue blackness he allegedly sought to cover with white polish. The October issue of *Mother Jones* tells this tale. The magazine's cover features an abstract color illustration of a grossly distorted O. J. Simpson, whose grotesque features are those of a monster. The cover story, "Killing Love"—a personal reflection on race, sex, and rage by Barbara Grizzuti Harrison—pronounces Simpson guilty in the same insidious way as the cover illustration: by abstract association.[51] The accompanying editorial by Jeffrey Klein, the editor-in-chief, is less heavy-handed in its presumption of guilt but still racially resonant. Klein writes compassionately of seeing O. J. and Nicole Simpson and their children laughing together on vacation just months before the murders. He speaks sympathetically of the man who seemingly remained unblemished amid the violence of the sport he played, who managed to build a Hall of Fame career on a losing team, and who presented the kind of image that big business wanted working on its behalf. But one of Klein's most poignant observations may say more than he intends about the relationship between race and ruin in America.

"When [Simpson] sprinted effortlessly through airports for Hertz cars," Klein writes, "focus groups said that they didn't perceive him as black. He was an All-American." But "America's color-blind perception of Simpson also meant no one really wanted to see the real O.J.; no wonder he lost sight of himself."[52] The real self is severely and profoundly black, but the national ethos is such that being black and being all-American are mutually exclusive. Klein's editorial is a thoughtful commentary on crime and punishment, but his words suggest just how much what ails America is a matter of who gets to be "American," and who gets to be American is still very much a matter not only of race but of color. Why couldn't O. J. Simpson be all-American *and* black?

"Despite his effort to rise above race," as *Newsweek* put it, Simpson "wound up in a kind of gilded no man's land"—neither white, as he tried to be, nor black like the homeboys he left behind, who said he was too white and further "scorned him for lusting after only white women."[53] The gilded no man's land (read "cage") in which Simpson wound up for fifteen months was a 7 × 9 jail cell, again a common destiny for black men. But while most of the nation and the world was ostensibly shocked that such a fate should befall so great a star, the presumptive racial narrative traced through the media would seem to suggest that this is essentially where this "polished hero with oddly jagged edges"[54] was headed all along. It appears, then, that even for a black American icon who would be white there is no end run around the squeeze play of race, the darker essential self. But if a touchdown can be called back, so too can a conviction. No matter how convinced of Simpson's guilt the media and much of the public may have been, the empaneled jury, in what many insist was a racial end run of its own, found O. J. Simpson not guilty of the crime of murder, after deliberating less than four hours.

If He Hollers, Let Him Go

Despite the jury verdict, the presumption of Simpson's guilt has prevailed. Moreover, the discrepancy between the presumptions of press and populace and the findings of the jury has inspired outrage among many white Americans in particular. "We expected more blacks to look beyond race to facts, as many whites had during the Rodney King trial," one *Newsweek* columnist wrote after the verdict. "When so many blacks didn't, it shocked us—and hardened us in ways that shocked us even more."[55]

It is important to understand that it was not black Rodney King who was on trial in the infamous case to which the columnist alludes, but four white police officers accused of beating King senseless. Nor were the facts of the Simpson case ever as incontrovertible as the videotape that caught the cops in the act of clubbing, kicking, and otherwise brutalizing a black male suspect. At the point that Marcia Clark and company rested their case, hordes of white lawyers, legal experts, columnists, and correspondents found the prosecution's facts so fraught and the burden of proof so insufficiently met that they ridiculed Simpson's dream team for even bothering to put on a defense. Conventional legal wisdom held that the defense should simply have rested. This judgment was offered, it is important to note, weeks before the Fuhrman tapes and the former detective's proven racism and perjured testimony further muddied the prosecution's case. Yet, at the end of the day, many of the same experts who had themselves gained fame and fortune by finding holes in the prosecution's mountain of evidence condemned the jury for its unreasonable doubt. It was easier, it seems, to blame this particular reversal of fortune on the black jurors' racial allegiance than on the systemic racism, tainted evidence, and perjured testimony that left room for doubt.

Few dared say it outright in print (except perhaps on the Internet), but the import of the hue and cry in the mainstream media and among the white masses was unmistakable: O. J. Simpson, through his eloquent mouthpiece Johnnie Cochran, hollered racism and a bunch of ignorant colored people let the nigger go. What's more, millions of blacks cheered this flagrant affront to the judicial system, as reasonable men and women looked on in horror and disgust, experiencing what *Newsweek* described as "white anguish" over the notion that "race can trump *both* class and gender"—that "a murderer [can] be a hero."[56]

Simpson is most certainly a batterer, but he is also, by the letter of the law, not a murderer. And neither is he, even for many of those who applauded his release, a hero. What many African Americans cheered was less the acquittal of Simpson, the wife beater and accused murderer, than the seeming reversal of the eeny-meeny-miny-mo double standard of justice that historically has held blacks not simply by the toe but by the throat; not above the law, like white men of wealth and influence, but beneath it, subject to its punishment but outside its protection. Among African Americans—who by no means received the verdict with the monolithic glee suggested by the strategically staged media moments[57]—reactions to the acquittal may say less about Simpson's perceived innocence than about the deep cynicism with which most black Americans regard the criminal justice system. Many white Americans—particularly in the wake of Rodney King—are willing to acknowledge in the abstract that justice is not blind to race or gender. Apparently, many are less willing to confront the dirty details of how racism taints everything it touches, including mountains of evidence.

But what made the Simpson verdict so second-guessable, so publicly assailable, is not doubts about the color biases of the legal system but assumptions about the colored and gendered bodies of the particular players. Here I want to cite not just the predominantly black jury, whose members were judged incapable of reason[58] long before they delivered their "irrational," "emotional," "inexplicable" verdict with "unseemly haste," but also the marginal cast of characters more generally: that is to say, the "hysterical," "strident" white woman and the "comic" colored men who litigated the trial of the century, bringing both disorder and dishonor to the court. Let me spell out what I mean.

Throughout the trial, many of us who followed the proceedings longed for the iron gavel of Judge Joseph Wapner of *The People's Court,* the investigative precision and perfection of Jack Klugman as TV medical examiner Dr. Quincy, and the infallible and always ethical legal wizardry of Raymond Burr as defense attorney Perry Mason. Judge Lance Ito (without a gavel at all), Dr. Lakshmanan Sathyavagiswaran (chief coroner for the county, whose Indian surname was deemed too long either to spell or pronounce), and Johnnie Cochran (black, sharp, successful) were poor substitutes. What our nostalgia for Wapner,

Quincy, and Mason may represent, however, is not just our latent desires for the quick-fix, murder-will-out resolutions of television but our unfamiliarity and ultimate discomfort with anything other than the white male authority that usually rules the courtroom and metes out justice.

Judge Ito lives in the press and popular imagination as the ineffectual, media-crazed captain of a multicultural ship of fools that spent nine months and nine million dollars running the judicial system aground. And, like the blackening of O. J. Simpson, the characterization of the judge is not without racial overtones. Not only did New York Republican senator Alfonse D'Amato make public fun of "little Judge Eeeee-toe" over the airwaves, endowing the American judge with a mock Japanese accent, but the terms in which Ito was often described by the media—lax, ineffectual, dithering, dilatory, indulgent, permissive, inept, star-struck, fawning, overly courteous—evoke the stereotype of the Asian man as an effeminate, obsequious wimp. The portrait was fleshed out by images of Ito teary-eyed at insults to his wife, reports of his ushering media celebrities such as Geraldo Rivera into his chambers, and news of his fawning over his own image reproduced fivefold in Jay Leno's "Dancing Itos." Alfonse D'Amato was hardly alone in accusing the judge of "making a disgrace of the judicial system": news magazines, tabloids, talk-show hosts, and fellow jurists issued similar indictments. After the trial, Robert Shapiro, hardly camera-shy himself, told Barbara Walters that Ito, like some of the lawyers, was seduced by the media, while co-counsel Peter Neufeld complained to *Time* that Ito not only entertained media personalities in his chambers but also told the lawyers Simpson jokes and showed them clips of the Dancing Itos and other TV skits. "As someone who has tried cases for 20 years," Neufeld said, "I found it deplorable, and I was shocked."[59]

Not long after Lance Ito was named to preside over the Simpson trial, an irate female viewer called in to *Rivera Live* to ask the host and his panel of legal experts why a Jap whose wife was high-placed in the LAPD had been chosen to hear the case.

Couldn't they find an American judge, she asked, or even an African American one? Geraldo and his guests rushed to explain that, while they had the option of asking Ito to recuse himself, both the prosecution and the defense wanted him to try the case because he was known to be a fair, good judge. As I recall, neither Geraldo nor any of his guests commented on the caller's use of "Jap" or on the way in which her question placed Ito outside the category "American."

Ito is certainly not beyond criticism or even attack. Nor do I mean to suggest that any criticism of a minority is automatically racist. What I want to uncover here, though, is the extent to which he, like Simpson and many of the key and bit players in this drama, is firmly fixed—prefixed, really or, given the Hollywood connection, typecast—in racial (and gender) ideologies. Perhaps no one but an anonymous caller would dare publicly hail Ito as a "Jap," but such name calling is hardly necessary because his yellow-peril Asianness is at least as already written as Simpson's true-blue blackness. Yet to the extent that the judge's essential Japaneseness is wimpy rather than warlike, it is also comic. Where Simpson is the commodity fetish, Ito is the comedy fetish, and his iconic agent is a Jell-O mold.[60] Presented with such an already drawn self-portrait, Ito may have elected to laugh with the media and the masses to cut the sting of being laughed at, of being a national joke. But how sad for him and for all of us that wearing judicial robes no more entitles him to the respect of the office than being born in the USA entitles him to be American.

Almost everything about this case and trial was—to use Peter Neufeld's terminology—deplorable and shocking, but the subtle message of much of the coverage and characterization of the players—the court jesters—may be that authorizing "others" in the court leads to what headlines in almost every publication called "disorder in the court." The same foreign, colored bodies who represent disorder in the culture bring chaos and mirth to the courtroom. Entrusted with Founding Father Law, they bypass Pharaoh and let their own people go. Despite the disruptive presence of her own much maligned white female body, this seems to be the verdict of Marcia Clark. "A majority black jury will never convict in a case like this," CNN reported her as saying after the not-guilty verdict. (Her office insisted she was misquoted, but the cable network stood by its report.) Contrary to fact as it is, such a charge presumes all blacks guilty of Negro nepotism and, therefore, unfit for jury duty and citizenship.

The presumption of innocence, which I have argued was never in force in the Simpson case, matters most in the court of law. In the court of public opinion, private citizens are entitled to their own views. But what of the media—reporters, correspondents, columnists, newscasters, lawyers, legal experts, talk-show hosts—or critics, scholars, and intellectuals, anyone who holds forth in public forums? Does our right to free speech, along with the public's right to know, supersede the accused's right to the presumption of innocence, to a fair trial, to proof beyond a reasonable doubt, to be *not guilty?* And, if so, what are the constitutional grounds for and the moral consequences of this ordering of rights?

In the Simpson case, the relevant criteria were not citizenship and its rights and privileges, as the Constitution dictates, but wealth and celebrity, on the one hand, and skin color, on the other. Although the former might portend presumptive innocence, the latter carries with it a historical supposition of guilt. To put a finer edge on my point, Simpson's black skin and racial past were already witnesses against him in the discursive production of guilt. The consequences of this construction—this overproduction—of guilt were most keenly felt in the aftershock of the not-guilty verdict. After fifteen months of gorging on the facts and fictions of the case, masses of media-fed Americans—whites particularly but by no means exclusively—were left with no doubt, reasonable or otherwise, of the defendant's guilt. For them, the verdict—perhaps even more so than the murders themselves—is a tragedy that flies in the face of reason, truth, justice, and the American way.

Certainly the real tragedy here must be the awful, sometimes forgotten slaughter of Nicole Brown Simpson and Ronald Goldman. But the specifically *American* tragedy may well be the fact that the nation's racist rather than romantic history allows for an easy conflation of the general and the particular. In general, race and racism have been the evil spirits denying African Americans equal justice under the law. Many Americans continue to insist, however, that in this particular case the race card was not the sinister black ace of spades that has helped to convict innocent black men, but a trump card that let a guilty man go free. Either way, it is an unspeakably devastating commentary on the roles, meanings, and consequences of race in a would-be colorblind society.

Epilogue

The More Bitter the Whine

> I loved history as a child, until some clear-eyed young Negro
> pointed out, quite rightly, that there was no place in the American
> past that I could go and be free.
>
> —Sherley Anne Williams, author's note in *Dessa Rose*

In June 1995 my youngest nephew graduated from my own small-town high school. Attending the event not only took me back to my hometown and my old school; it also carried me back, with considerable nostalgia, to my commencement twenty-eight years earlier. It was 1967, *the sixties,* the Age of Aquarius. Nixon was not yet in the Whitehouse, and though all was far from well with the world, we believed we could make it so. Despite the fact that both Malcolm X and John F. Kennedy—each in his own way a beacon of a new day—had died violent deaths not long before, the Camelot of the Kennedys and the Promised Land of Martin Luther King still loomed on the horizon. And we were hopeful, dazzled by our own dreams and propelled by the promise of what lay ahead: liberty, equality, justice, and—as we waged war on poverty—even prosperity for all.

We didn't know then that within the year Martin Luther King would be dead. We didn't know as we marched into the auditorium with "Pomp and Circumstance," resplendent in our gowns of green and white and in our hope, that Robert Kennedy—the heir apparent to Camelot, who promised to take us there with him—would also be gunned down before the dust could settle on our diplomas. Both men talked in terms of dreams. For King, it was the dream of a Promised Land in which the sons (and daughters) of former slaves and the sons (and daughters) of former slaveholders would walk hand in hand. Kennedy, quoting the poet, was fond of saying: "Some men see things as they are and ask 'why?'; I dream dreams that never were and ask 'why not?'" We, that is, those of my generation and inclination—the radical children of the sixties, the baby boomers—dreamed along with Kennedy and King. And some—freedom riders, war protesters, civil rights activists, Black Panthers, Gray Panthers, Gay Panthers—laid down their lives for those dreams.

Despite the current regressive political climate, I do not mean to suggest that the men, women, and schoolchildren who lost their lives in pursuit of these dreams died in vain. I am able to write and publish these words today because of them. I teach at institutions where, but for their challenges to the "natural" order of things, I would not be. Yet it is painfully clear that the better part of the promised land of liberty, equality, and justice for all—the better part of a Camelot of peaceful coexistence and prosperity—remains, for the majority of Americans, a dream deferred. As Langston Hughes warned, a dream too long deferred is a dream likely to explode.

We have felt the aftershocks of exploded dreams several times: for one, the conflagration in Los Angeles that followed the acquittal of the police officers charged with beating Rodney King. Whereas the media attempted to reduce what happened in the city to a race riot—a conflict between white and black, between the law and the lawless—many understood that what actually occurred in April 1992 was, to paraphrase Cornel West, a multiracial, interethnic, transclass display of seething social rage.[1] More recently, discontent and rage led to firestorms and multiple deaths in Waco, Ruby Ridge, and Oklahoma City. White rage and racial hatred are believed by many to be the inspiration behind the burning and bombing of black churches throughout the South. Thirty-two predominantly black churches have gone up in flames since 1989.

For all our hopes and dreams, this is the legacy that my generation seems to be leaving the next: not Camelot but the country ablaze (and not with a thousand points of light), not a promised land of equal opportunity where the living is decent for everyone, but a desert of economic decline and cultural decay, where the living is deadly for many. We leave behind a country where ethnic rivalry, race hatred, bigotry, antisemitism, sexism, heterosexism, and even neo-Nazism are on the rise, as the economically disadvantaged, the politically disenfranchised, the overtaxed working and middle classes, and the privileged elite fight for increasingly smaller pieces of an increasingly smaller pie.

For Newt Gingrich and others whom the Statue of Liberty has smiled on, America may well be a series of romantic folktales that happen to be true. But for the country's castoffs—descendants of the removed, the enslaved, the excluded, and the interned—the nation's past and, more important, its present are anything but romantic. The gap between the American dream and the stark realities of life for most Americans is a source of escalating disillusionment and anger. It is the energy behind a politically empowered backlash that blames "the other" for the nation's woes and has already begun to dismantle many of the affirmative action, antidiscrimination, and social welfare programs so hard won in the sixties. It is the force behind a bitter and prophetic whine that reverberates throughout the country, from the fruited plains of the nation's heartland to the legislative chambers of the nation's capital.

Whatever hope there is for America lies not in a romantic return to the days of yesteryear—whether the site is the sixties of my imagination or the New Republic of Newt Gingrich's. Whatever chance America has to survive whole as a nation rests in a head-on collision with the deep structures and historical roots of its social and economic problems. This means owning up to our sins. It means decoding rather than denying the country's entrenched schemes of color, class, and gender. It means acknowledging racism as a fundamental element of the American condition, from the seeming innocence of Barbie dolls to the assumed guilt of O. J. Simpson, from interpersonal relationships to public policy. As long as people—especially people in power—continue to believe that our country has "no caste system, no class requirements, no regulated professions, no barriers to entry,"[2] America will remain a deeply divided society with an ever-widening gap between the haves and the have-nots, between men and women, between white and black, between All-Americans and niggers, between the whiteface of Timothy McVeigh and the blackface of O. J. Simpson. The best thing we can do for ourselves and our country—the best contract we can make with America—is exactly to deromanticize it. Given all the crises we face, not to do this is to take out a contract on America.

Du Bois was right: the problem of the twentieth century has indeed been the color line, and there is every reason to believe that it will be the problem of the twenty-first century as well. Perhaps somewhere over the rainbow there is a land where equality and justice are colorblind, where no one is the other, where no one by virtue of race, gender, or sexual orientation is an outcast or an anomaly. In the real world, however, it would seem that racism, sexism, and heterosexism are permanent features of the human condition. But accepting these facts of American life as both a legacy from the past and a bequest to the future does not mean that we should give up our pursuit of that best of all possible worlds beyond the rainbow. It means that we have to be all the more vigilant in cultivating our gardens or, closer to reality, our briarpatches.

Notes

Prologue

1. See Tom Morganthau, "What Color Is Black?" *Newsweek,* February 13, 1995, p. 64.

2. "The O. J. Simpson Industry," *Investigative Reports,* Arts and Entertainment Television Networks, July 21, 1995.

3. Newt Gingrich, *To Renew America* (New York: HarperCollins, 1995), p. 30.

4. Thomas Jefferson, *Notes on the State of Virginia* (1782), in Harvey Wish, ed., *Slavery in the South* (New York: Farrar, Straus, and Giroux, 1970), p. 224; later quotations on pp. 224–225, 231.

5. Gingrich, *To Renew America,* pp. 33–34. Later quotations on pp. 30, 32.

6. James H. Johnson Jr. and Walter C. Farrell Jr., "Race Still Matters," *Chronicle of Higher Education,* July 7, 1995, p. A48. In this fascinating report, Johnson and Farrell point out that although a criminal record also affects employability, race and skin color are more relevant than such cultural factors as growing up in a welfare-dependent household. The fact that a police record is a major deterrent to getting a job is significant, the scholars explain, because of the national obsession with punishment and because of racial disparities in the degree of punishment imposed for similar offenses. Possession of five grams of crack-cocaine, the drug most commonly used by inner-city blacks, carries a federally mandated five-year minimum sentence—without the possibility of parole; but possession of the same amount of powdered cocaine, the drug of choice among middle- and upper-class whites, is a misdemeanor that carries a one-year maximum sentence.

7. According to media reports, the message was spread across several pages of the 1995 Greenwich High School yearbook and might have gone

undiscovered if one of the perpetrators had not bragged to friends about the coup he and four classmates had pulled off.

1. Toy Theory

1. See Sarah and A. Elizabeth Delany, *Having Our Say: The Delany Sisters' First 100 Years* (New York: Kodansha, 1993), p. 69.

2. In focusing on some of the hurts of childhood, I don't mean to suggest that there were no joys. I would do my white classmates an injustice if I did not also acknowledge that many of them and their families were never anything but kind to me.

3. It is only in watching late-night reruns of the old shows from the fifties that I realize that my hero Perry Mason never defended and rarely encountered anyone who was not white. African Americans appeared in these shows only on rare occasions and usually only as porters, janitors, butlers, and maids. Asians, if memory serves me correctly, made occasional appearances either as inscrutably wise jade merchants or as villains.

4. It's not that I consciously thought of him as white but that he was conceived in the image of such tall, dark, and handsome white men as John Gavin, who played opposite Susan Hayward in the tearjerker *Back Street*, and Debbie Reynolds's leading man in *Tammy and the Bachelor*. As a child of eight in 1957, I thought Tammy's bachelor was to die for. Only recently did I realize that the man I found so handsome then was none other than Leslie Nielson of *Naked Gun* fame. *Tammy* had a special significance for me because we saw it at the drive-in with our friends who were visiting from Atlanta. Their daughter, an only child, was a little older than I. She seemed to have everything any child could want, but because of segregation she had never been to a drive-in movie. The right to see *Tammy* at the drive-in was the one thing I had over her. When she bragged about her father's new car, I countered that I, unlike her, could see *Tammy* or any other movie whenever I wanted. And then I would break into the song, "I hear the cottonwoods whispering above / Ta-a-mmy, Ta-a-mmy, Tammy's in love."

5. Kathy Russell, Midge Wilson, and Ronald Hall, *The Color Complex: The Politics of Skin Color among African Americans* (New York: Anchor Books, 1992), p. 41.

6. Michele Wallace, "Modernism, Postmodernism and the Problem of the Visual in Afro-American Culture," in Russell Ferguson, Martha Gever, Trinh T. Minh-ha, and Cornel West, eds., *Out There: Marginalization and Contemporary Cultures* (New York and Cambridge: New Museum of Contemporary Art and MIT Press, 1992), p. 40.

7. My mother lived with the Halyards for eight and a half years, from

the time she was seven until she was fifteen. She never reported their abusive behavior, not even Mr. Halyard's sexual advances, which began when she was about thirteen. I tell this story not only with her blessing but somewhat at her behest, as a way of bearing witness. My mother has often said that no matter what they did to her she was grateful to the Halyards for giving her a home. I could never be that forgiving. As fostercare providers in the employ of the state, the Halyards were paid for my mother's upkeep and maintenance. I grew up hating the name Halyard; it was for me synonymous with Devil.

8. One of my favorite stories was the one about the white male supervisor at Raytheon who dared to shake his fist at my mother because she refused to run two complicated machines at the same time, while two of her white women coworkers sat around doing simple busy work. I could barely wait for my mother to get to the part in the story where she called her supervisor a stupid little pipsqueak, grabbed her hat, coat, and time-card, and punched out. Some of her coworkers reported the incident to the shop steward, which led to an investigation by the union. Management wanted my mother to sign a paper saying that she had been insubordinate. She said she'd be glad to, as soon as they signed one saying that they were prejudiced. She pointed not only to her own case but to that of a black coworker named Mildred Jenkins. Jenkins, my mother said, had been passed over for a position she was well qualified to fill; the job was given to a white woman with much less seniority. Mildred Jenkins got the promotion she deserved, what she called her "Pearl duCille job."

9. The term "ethnically correct" frequently appears in discussions of ethnic Barbie dolls and other would-be multicultural toys. The earliest usage I have come across is in an article, "Remco: Negro Girls Want 'Realistic' Dolls," which appeared in the July 1968 issue of *Playthings*, a trade publication. The term was repeated in a 1976 press release about Shindana Toys—a black-owned company founded in the late 1960s —whose president, Robert Bobo, described his company's dolls as "ethnically correct," with real "Negroid features." The term is one I want to problematize.

10. Dressed by Bob Mackie, painted by Andy Warhol, Barbie has become an increasingly popular topic for the media. Phil Donahue, Oprah, and other talk shows have devoted entire programs to Barbie collecting. The doll has been much written about in the popular press—from a front-page story in the *Boston Globe* to editorials and features in the *New York Times, Time,* and *Newsweek.* As signifiers of the anorexia that killed the singer Karen Carpenter, Barbie dolls were cast in starring roles in Todd Haynes's 1987 documentary film *Superstar: The Karen Carpenter Story.* The doll also makes an appearance in Barbara Kingsolver's novel *Pigs in*

Heaven (1993), and it is the focal figure in a collection of poems, short stories, and vignettes entitled *Mondo Barbie* (1993). Barbie has also caught the attention of academics. In recent years, the doll has been the subject of papers delivered at the Berkshire Conference on Women and at the annual meetings of the Modern Language Association, the American Studies Association, and the College Art Association. The feminist scholar Susan Willis devotes part of a chapter to Barbie in *A Primer for Daily Life* (New York: Routledge, 1988). M. G. Lord, a syndicated columnist, has written a biography, *Forever Barbie: The Unauthorized Biography of a Real Doll* (New York: Morrow, 1994). Erica Rand, an art historian who teaches at Bates College, has published a book entitled *Barbie's Queer Accessories* (Durham: Duke University Press, 1995) about the subversive uses to which Barbie is put, including the doll's presence in gay and lesbian culture. Mel McCombie, also an art historian, has written several articles and given a number of talks about Barbie, fashion, body image, and teenage culture.

11. Ruth Handler, who came up with the idea for the doll and thinks of herself as Barbie's mother, has had much to say about the Barbie doll as a role model. This particular quotation is taken from a booklet that comes with 35th Anniversary Barbie, an "authentic reproduction" of the first Barbie dolls sold in 1959. Handler, by the way, named Barbie after her daughter Barbara and Ken after her son.

12. In her biography of Barbie, Lord maintains that the original dolls were given undergarments because Charlotte Johnson, Barbie's first dress designer, insisted that a fashion doll couldn't wear haute-couture ensembles without the proper foundations. *Forever Barbie,* p. 34.

13. See BillyBoy, *Barbie: Her Life and Times* (New York: Crown, 1987), p. 22. Barbie herself would seem to agree with BillyBoy. In *Barbie: What a Doll!* "by Barbie, as told to Laura Jacobs" (New York: Abbeville Press, 1994), the putative author informs her readers: "In the early 1960s, when fashions required more elaborate foundations like girdles and garters (before pantyhose had come along), my repertoire of intimate apparel was a bit more various. But as feminism and fashion together moved women away from a standardized ideal of perfection and toward a more embracing acceptance of fitness and its many different physiques, we no longer needed undergarments that would shape everyone the same way . . . A figure was now akin to a fingerprint; no two bodies wore the same dress the same way" (p. 75).

14. Greta Slobin, personal conversation, December 14, 1994.

15. Ingeborg Majer O'Sickey, "*Barbie Magazine* and the Aesthetic Commodification of Girls' Bodies," in Shari Benstock and Suzanne Ferriss, eds., *On Fashion* (New Brunswick: Rutgers University Press, 1994), pp. 21–40, esp. p. 23.

16. Anna Quindlen, "Barbie at 35," *New York Times,* September 10, 1994, p. 19.

17. Helen Cordes, "What a Doll! Barbie: Materialistic Bimbo or Feminist Trailblazer?," *Utne Reader,* March-April 1992, p. 50.

18. Among the 270 phrases programmed into the computer chip of some editions of Teen Talk Barbie in 1992 was "Math class is tough." This drew protests from a variety of sources, including formal complaints from the National Council of Teachers of Mathematics, the Association for Women in Mathematics, and the American Association of University Women. Mattel, not wanting to convey "anything but the most inspirational of messages," promptly removed the offending phrase from Barbie's microchip. See Tony Kornheiser, "Shut Up, Barbie," *Washington Post,* October 4, 1992, p. F1. See also Constance Holden, "Mathematicians Talk Tough to New Barbie," *Science* 258 (1992), 396; and "No More Math Phobia for Barbie," *New York Times,* October 2, 1994, p. 28.

19. Karen Sanchez-Eppler, *Touching Liberty: Abolition, Feminism, and the Politics of the Body* (Berkeley: University of California Press, 1993), p. 133.

20. Both my own research and that of others reveal that Barbie dolls are frequently sexual subjects in children's play. Many adult women have told me that what they habitually did with Ken and Barbie was to make them "have sex," even when the details of "having sex" were not understood. Others have expressed disdain for the anatomical incorrectness of Ken in particular. "Who'd they think they were kidding?" one woman—now a college professor—asked me. "I had brothers. I knew what boys looked like. Where's his peter? That's what I wanted to know."

21. Mel McCombie, "Toys R Us" (unpublished paper), p. 4.

22. Ken was introduced in 1961. According to Lord, a battle raged at Mattel over Ken's genitals. Ruth Handler and Charlotte Johnson argued for giving Ken a "bulge" or a "bump," while the male executives reportedly were embarrassed even by the idea of an implied penis. A slight bump was the compromise. *Forever Barbie,* pp. 48–50.

23. A manifesto circulated by something called the Committee to Arm Barbie argues that, given the prevalence of violence against women, Barbie dolls should come with guns instead of ball gowns.

24. According to an article in the *Washington Post,* Nancy Reagan's fondness for designer dresses and fine china caused her to finish next to last in a poll of historians asked to rank first ladies. (Mary Todd Lincoln, who held seances in the White House and bought 300 pairs of gloves in four months, took last place.) Nancy Reagan "became a symbol of the uncaring rich, a Barbie doll with an attitude," the article says. See Eleanor Clif, "Nancy Reagan Shined as an Effective First Lady," rpt. in *Hartford Courant,* January 17, 1995, p. All.

25. See Sheila Parker, Mimi Nichter, Mark Nichter, Nancy Vuckovic, Colette Sims, and Cheryl Ritenbaugh, "Body Image and Weight Concerns among African American and White Adolescent Females: Differences Which Make a Difference," report compiled in 1994 at the University of Arizona, Tucson. In addition to detailing the results of a number of nationwide surveys, this report uses data collected from a multiethnic study of female adolescents to explore the factors that affect perceptions of weight, body, beauty, and style. I am grateful to Mimi Nichter and her colleagues for providing me with access to this paper in advance of its publication.

26. *ABC Nightly News,* August 28, 1994. In the video, a human Barbie and an animated version of plastic Barbie lead an interracial cast of nine girls in thirty minutes of dance exercise. According to the label, the video has been approved by the Aerobics and Fitness Association of America.

27. Mimi Nichter and Nancy Vuckovic, "Fat Talk: Body Image among Adolescent Girls," in Nicole Sault, ed., *Many Mirrors: Body Image and Social Relations* (New Brunswick: Rutgers University Press, 1994), pp. 116, 128n3. Informants came from lower- and upper-middle-class families; 73 percent of the informants were Caucasian, 16 percent Hispanic, and 11 percent African American or Asian American (pp. 110–111).

28. But even these findings have a rough edge. Studies show that while they may be less concerned about weight, African American girls also tend to see themselves as thinner than they are. This has potentially serious implications, both because there is a high incidence of obesity among African American women and because African American women are less inclined to view being overweight as unhealthy. See Parker, Nichter, et al., "Body Image," pp. 1–5. I wonder to what extent these findings might be inflected by variables such as class, community, and locale. Are African American girls less preoccupied with weight and dieting in general, or do attitudes about body image differ according to situation? Would a black girl growing up in a white environment, as I did, be more likely to view herself in relation to African American girls outside her peer group or in relation to her white peers? Other research suggests, by the way, that "fat talk" and concern about body image are not limited to girls and women.

29. Becky W. Thompson, *A Hunger So Wide and So Deep: American Women Speak Out on Eating Problems* (Minneapolis: University of Minnesota Press, 1994), p. 9. Thompson employs the term "eating problem" rather than the more widely used "eating disorder," which "suggests that some psychological frailty or inadequacy is the agent of the illness" (p. 1).

30. Christopher Crowfield [Harriet Beecher Stowe], *The Chimney Corner* (Boston, 1868), quoted in Lois W. Banner, *American Beauty* (Chicago: University of Chicago Press, 1983), p. 47.

31. Banner, *American Beauty*, p. 290.

32. Until 1950 rule 7 of the regulations governing the Miss America pageant stated that contestants had to be in good health and of the white race. According to *Miss America: Beyond the Crown*—a historical, behind-the-scenes look at the pageant that aired on NBC on September 10, 1994—Miss America 1950 was instrumental in getting this regulation changed. The documentary included an interview with Kimberly Aiken, who, with tears running down her cheeks, spoke of what it meant for her as a black woman to wear the crown, having watched the pageant as a child with her mother and grandmother, who could not even imagine the possibility of a black Miss America.

33. Banner, *American Beauty*, pp. 289–290.

34. Although the subject of the essay is initially referred to only as Happy, the doll pictured pre-surgery appears to be the one marketed as Happy To Be Me by a company called High Self Esteem Toys of Woodbury, Minnesota. The fact that the article cites Woodbury as Happy's place of residence also suggests that Happy To Be Me is the target. The link between Barbie and plastic surgery is also confirmed by Cindy Jackson, founder of the London Cosmetic Surgery Network, who has had more than twenty surgical procedures (including three facelifts, three chemical peels, two nose jobs, and—she boasts—a "boob job" paid for by the BBC) in her quest to look like Barbie.

35. Ivan Burton, "Happy to Be Midge," *Barbie Bazaar* 6 (January-February 1994), 53–54.

36. Lord, *Forever Barbie*, p. 227.

37. Lord also points out that Happy To Be Me was poorly designed and cheaply made, with ill-fitting clothes that bunched in unflattering ways. These flaws, she argues, contributed to the doll's failure in the marketplace. *Forever Barbie*, pp. 228–229.

38. Susan Willis, *A Primer for Daily Life* (New York: Routledge, 1991), p. 23. Willis, paraphrasing Marx, defines the commodity form as "the negation of process and the social relations of production."

39. Barbara Kantrowitz, "Hot Date: Barbie and G.I. Joe," *Newsweek*, February 20, 1989, pp. 59–60.

40. Alice Dembner, "Thirty-Five and Still a Doll," *Boston Globe*, March 9, 1994, pp. 1, 16.

41. Donna Larcen, "Barbie Bond Doesn't Diminish with Age," *Hartford Courant*, August 17, 1993, pp. A6–7.

42. Cindy Yoon, "A Doll of Our Own," *A Magazine (Asian American Quarterly)*, September 1994, p. 28.

43. Kitturah B. Westenhauser, *The Story of Barbie* (Paducah, Kentucky: Collector Books, 1994), p. 23.

44. Cynthia Roberts, *Barbie: Thirty Years of America's Doll* (Chicago: Contemporary Books, 1989), p. 44.

45. Westenhauser, *The Story of Barbie*, p. 136.

46. See Myla Perkins, *Black Dolls: An Identification and Value Guide, 1820–1991* (Paducah, Kentucky: Collector Books, 1993), pp. 246–249. See also Westenhauser, pp. 134–136, and Lord, pp. 160–171. While they do give considerable credit to black community leaders Lou Smith and Robert Hall, both Westenhauser and Lord make Mattel the primary heroes behind the founding and early management of Shindana Toys. Perkins acknowledges the initial technical and financial support of the Mattel Corporation, but points out that this black enterprise was the dream of black community leaders Smith and Hall, the cofounders of Operation Bootstrap. While Mattel certainly aided Shindana in getting its own line of black dolls off the ground—or, more correctly, out of the ashes of Watts—Mattel also rushed its own black doll onto the market, indeed making itself Shindana's "competitor." History may be poised to repeat itself in the escalating competition between Mattel and Olmec Toys, a black-owned corporation founded in 1985.

47. Remco Toys also introduced four "ethnically correct" black dolls at the 1968 Toy Fair.

48. According to Westenhauser, the white Steffie doll, whose face mold remains popular, was itself shortlived, remaining on the market only from 1972 to 1973. Her head mold, however, "typifies the flexibility that slight alterations of the facial paint can have on marketability" (p. 24).

49. Roberts, *Barbie*, p. 92.

50. This quotation, too, is taken from the special edition booklet that comes packaged with 35th Anniversary Barbie.

51. Roberts, *Barbie*, p. 92.

52. Perkins, *Black Dolls*, pp. 248–249. Perkins reprints the text of the 1976 press release issued from the public relations firm of Harshe-Rotman and Druck.

53. David N. Berkwitz, "Finally, Barbie Doll Ads Go Ethnic," *Newsweek*, August 13, 1990, p. 48.

54. Ibid., p. 48.

55. Catherine Belsey, *Critical Practice* (New York: Routledge, 1987), p. 47.

56. According to various doll-collector magazines, handmade, one-of-a-kind, and limited-edition dolls made by doll artists range in price from several hundred dollars to as much as $20,000.

57. Part of Article I, section 2, of the U.S. Constitution established that only three-fifths of a state's slave population would be counted in determining a state's congressional representation and federal tax share. Passed by

California voters in November 1994, Proposition 187 sought to deny undocumented immigrants access to public education and health care.

58. Dan Savage, "Ken Comes Out," *Chicago Reader,* Summer 1993, p. 8.

59. Richard Roeper, *Chicago Sun Times,* August 3, 1993, p. 11.

60. Telephone conversation with Donna Gibbs, September 9, 1994.

61. Mattel denies that Earring Magic Ken was pulled from the market. He was simply part of a 1993 Barbie line that was discontinued, a spokesperson told me. Some toystore managers and clerks tell a different story, however.

62. Phone conversation with Gibbs, September 9, 1994.

63. Sibyl DeWein and Joan Ashabraner, *The Collectors Encyclopedia of Barbie Dolls and Collectibles* (Paducah: Collector Books, 1994), p. 35.

64. This is the price range listed in the 11th edition of Jan Foulke's *Blue Book: Dolls and Values* (Grantsville, Md.: Hobby House Press, 1993), p. 83. Many of what are called vintage dolls—early or otherwise special-edition Barbie dolls—have the "premium value" described by Donna Gibbs. For example, according to the *Blue Book* a first-edition 1959 Barbie never removed from its box would be worth between $3,200 and $3,700. A Barbie infomercial airing in 1994–95 placed the value as high as $4,500. The same doll sold in 1959 for $2.99.

65. Westenhauser, *Story of Barbie,* pp. 138, 119. Serious Barbie collectors often purchase duplicates of a given doll: one to keep in mint condition in its box and one to display. Or, as we used to say of the two handkerchiefs we carried to Sunday school: one for show and one for blow. For an intriguing psychosocial analysis of the art of collecting, see Jean Baudrillard, "The System of Collecting," in John Elsner and Roger Cardinal, eds., *The Cultures of Collecting* (Cambridge, Mass.: Harvard University Press, 1994), pp. 7–24.

66. After many calls to the Jamaican embassy in Washington and to various cultural organizations in Jamaica, I have concluded that Jamaican Barbie's costume—a floor-length granny dress with apron and head-rag—bears some resemblance to what is considered the island's traditional folk costume. But it was also made clear to me that these costumes have more to do with tourism than with local traditions. According to Gibbs at Mattel, decisions about costuming are made by the design and marketing teams in consultation with other senior staffers. The attempt, Gibbs informed me, "is to determine and roughly approximate" the national costume of each country in the collection (conversation, September 9, 1994). I still wonder, though, about the politics of these design decisions: why the doll representing Jamaica is figured as a maid, while the doll representing Great Britain is presented as a lady—a blond, blue-eyed Barbie doll dressed in a fancy riding habit with boots and hat.

67. Actually, Jamaican *patois* is spelled differently: *potwah*, I believe.

68. See e.g. Morris Rosenberg, *Conceiving the Self* (New York: Basic Books, 1979) and *Society and the Adolescent Self-Image* (Hanover: University Press of New England, 1989), and William E. Cross, *Shades of Black: Diversity in African American Identity* (Philadelphia: Temple University Press, 1991), which challenge the Clarks' findings. The psychologist Na'im Akbar argues that just as the Moynihan Report pathologized the black family, the Clark doll studies pathologized the black community by the implied assumption that it was "psychologically unhealthy for 'colored' children to go to school only with one another,'" since "the outcome is likely to be self-hatred, lowered motivation, and so on." According to Akbar, this problematic assumption gave rise to a racist logical fallacy embedded in the 1954 Supreme Court decision: that it was "psychologically healthy for Black children to attend school with white children," since "such an opportunity is likely to improve the African-American child's self-concept, intellectual achievement, and overall social and psychological adjustment." Akbar, "Our Destiny: Authors of a Scientific Revolution," in Harriette Pipes McAdoo and John Lewis McAdoo, eds., *Black Children: Social, Educational, and Parental Environments* (Beverly Hills: Sage Publications, 1985), pp. 24–25. Akbar's analysis seems to miss the point that what concerned black parents in the 1950s (as well as before and since) was the material effects of Jim Crow education: separate was not equal.

69. Harriette Pipes McAdoo, "Racial Attitudes and Self Concept of Young Black Children over Time," in *Black Children*, p. 214.

70. Darlene Powell Hopson and Derek S. Hopson, *Different and Wonderful: Raising Black Children in a Race-Conscious Society* (New York: Simon and Schuster, 1990), pp. xix–xx.

71. Ibid., p. 127; my emphasis. *"You do not want your child to grow up thinking that only White dolls, and by extension White people, are attractive and nice,"* the Hopsons go on to explain (emphasis in the original).

72. The cover of the November-December 1993 issue of *Barbie* offers a good illustration of my point. It is dominated by a full-page image of white Happy Holiday Barbie. Tucked away in a tiny insert in the upper-left corner is the face of a black Barbie doll, presumably stuck in to let us know that Happy Holiday Barbie also comes in black. Black Barbie was the cover story in *Barbie Bazaar*, May-June 1996.

73. Hopson and Hopson, *Different and Wonderful*, pp. 119, 124.

74. It is also clear that other factors influenced Mattel's decision to go ethnic, including a marketing survey done in the late 1980s, which reportedly identified the top fourteen cities with the highest concentrations of black residents. According to the doll dealer and appraiser A. Glenn

Mandeville, Mattel used this information and the complaints and suggestions of consumers to help develop its Shani line. In his words, "Mattel has indeed gone out in the 1990s to make sure they capture all markets." *Doll Fashion Anthology and Price Guide*, 3rd ed. (Cumberland: Hobby House Press, 1992), p. 174.

75. Asha is a variant of the Swahili and Arabic name Aisha or Ayisha, meaning "life" or "alive." It is also the name of Muhammed's chief wife. As a minor point of interest, "Nichelle" is the first name of the black actress (Nichelle Nichols) who played Lieutenant Uhura on the original *Star Trek* TV series (1966–1969).

76. Quoted in Lisa Jones, "A Doll Is Born," *Village Voice*, March 26, 1991, p. 36.

77. Kenyan Barbie, introduced in 1994, has the most closely cropped hair of any Barbie doll to date. I asked Donna Gibbs if Mattel was concerned that the doll's severely cropped hair (little more than peach fuzz, or what a colleague described as "Afro turf") would hamper sales. She told me that the company expected Kenyan Barbie to sell as well as all the other national dolls, which are intended more for adult collectors. Kenyan Barbie received a "short-cropped Afro in an attempt to make her look more authentic," Gibbs informed me. "She represents a more authentic-looking doll." (The doll also has bare feet and wears Mattel's interpretation of the native dress of the Masai woman; the first-person narrative on the back of the box tells us that most Kenyan people wear modern dress and that spears are banned in the city.)

78. Gibbs, conversation, September 9, 1994.

79. See Gerald Early, "Life with Daughters: Watching the Miss America Pageant," in his *The Culture of Bruising: Essays on Prizefighting, Literature, and Modern American Culture* (Hopewell: Ecco Press, 1994), p. 268.

80. Among many texts on the politics of black people's hair, see Cheryl Clarke's poem "Hair: A Narrative," in her *Narratives: Poems in the Tradition of Black Women* (New York: Kitchen Table/Women of Color Press, 1982); Kobena Mercer, "Black Hair/Style Politics," in Ferguson, Gever, Minh-ha, and West, eds., *Out There*, pp. 247–264; and Ayoka Chinzera, director, *Hairpiece: A Film for Nappy-Headed People*, 1982. In fiction see Toni Morrison's *The Bluest Eye*.

81. I intend no value judgment in making this observation about what we do with our hair. Though Afros, braids, and dreadlocks may be seen by some as more "authentically black" or more Afrocentrically political than straightened or chemically processed hair, I am inclined to agree with Kobena Mercer that all black hairstyles are political as a historical ethnic signifier (p. 251). It is history that has made black hair "*mean*."

82. Mercer, "Black Hair/Style Politics," pp. 247–248.

83. Jacqueline Urla and Alan Swedlund, "The Anthropometry of Barbie: Unsettling Ideas of the Feminine in Popular Culture," in Jennifer Terry and Jacqueline Urla, eds., *Deviant Bodies: Critical Perspectives on Difference in Science and Popular Culture* (Bloomington: Indiana University Press, 1995).

84. Sander L. Gilman, "Black Bodies, White Bodies: Toward an Iconography of Female Sexuality in Late Nineteenth-Century Art, Medicine, and Literature," in Henry Louis Gates Jr., ed., *"Race," Writing, and Difference* (Chicago: University of Chicago Press, 1985), p. 238.

85. See Stephen Jay Gould, "The Hottentot Venus," *Natural History* 91 (1982), 20–27. For a poetic interpretation of Sarah Bartmann's story, see the title poem in Elizabeth Alexander's *The Venus Hottentot* (Charlottesville: University of Virginia Press, 1990), pp. 3–7.

86. Anne Fausto Sterling, "Gender, Race, and Nation: The Comparative Anatomy of 'Hottentot' Women in Europe: 1815–1817," in Terry and Urla, eds., *Deviant Bodies*, pp. 19–48.

87. Gilman, "Black Bodies, White Bodies," p. 232.

2. Monster, She Wrote

1. Lerone Bennett Jr., "The Roots of Black Love," *Ebony*, August 1981, pp. 31–36. Bennett exempts such writers as Paul Laurence Dunbar and such musicians as John Coltrane and the Commodores whom he sees as contributing to "the vitality of the Black love tradition" with poems such as "When Malindy Sings" and songs such as "Soul Eyes" and "Once, Twice, Three Times a Lady," all of which position black women not as active agents in history but as objects of male desire. "Careless Love," to which Bennett alludes in his essay, is an old song that Bessie Smith made famous. The poet Robert Hayden incorporates lyrics from "Careless Love" in his tribute to Smith, "Homage to the Empress of the Blues." Bennett may be referring to Hayden's poem as well as to the song itself. Zora Neale Hurston also incorporates lyrics from this "old, old ballad" in her last novel, *Seraph on the Suwanee* (1948).

2. See Deborah McDowell, "Reading Family Matters," in Cheryl Wall, ed., *Changing Our Own Words: Essays on Criticism, Theory, and Writing by Black Women* (New Brunswick: Rutgers University Press, 1989), pp. 75–97. Drawing on reviews and articles published primarily in the white literary media and popular press, McDowell brilliantly analyzes the vitriolic responses that the fiction of writers like Walker, Morrison, and Jones have inspired in black male critics, such as Mel Watkins and Darryl Pinckney.

Part of the problem, she points out, is that African American history has been written (by men) as a family romance in which black men battle not their women but the oppressive forces of white racism. In representing black male abuse within the family, black women writers are writing outside the family, against the family romance.

3. A number of black women writers labeled "feminists" by black male critics—Gayl Jones, for one—have not so identified themselves.

4. Don Alexander and Christine Wright, "Race, Sex and Class: The Clash over *The Color Purple*," *Women and Revolution* 34 (Spring 1988), 20.

5. McDowell, "Family Matters," pp. 75–76.

6. "Interview with Alice Walker," in John O'Brien, ed., *Interviews with Black Writers* (New York: Liveright, 1973), p. 192; Roseann P. Bell, "Judgment: Addison Gayle," in Bell, Bettye J. Parker, and Beverly Guy-Sheftall, eds., *Sturdy Black Bridges: Visions of Black Women in Literature* (Garden City: Anchor Books, 1979), p. 214; Ishmael Reed, *New Amsterdam News* (January-February 1987), quoted in Alexander and Wright, "Race, Sex and Class," p. 20.

7. Bell, "Addison Gayle," p. 214.

8. See e.g. Calvin C. Hernton, *The Sexual Mountain and Black Women Writers: Adventures in Sex, Literature and Real Life* (New York: Doubleday, 1987).

9. Black women's literature has acquired many champions among black male scholars. Some of these men's work presents a problem slightly different from the one I address here. Rather than denigrating feminism and its fictions, this criticism announces itself as feminist discourse, even as it remains male-identified. It is also worth noting that several black feminist critics—Barbara Smith, Ann Allen Shockley, and Jewelle Gomez, for example—have called attention to what has been either the absence of black lesbians in African American women's literature or the presence of negative representations of black lesbian experiences.

10. Bell, "Addison Gayle," p. 214.

11. Mel Watkins, "Sexism, Racism and Black Women Writers," *New York Times Book Review*, June 15, 1986, p. 36.

12. In the Foucauldian sense, "discursive formations" are fields of knowledge or concepts that privilege certain utterances while suppressing others.

13. W. Lawrence Hogue, "History, the Feminist Discourse, and *The Third Life of Grange Copeland*," chap. 5 in his *Discourse and the Other* (Durham: Duke University Press, 1986). Later quotations from pp. 104–105, 65.

14. In addition to noting that *The Third Life* necessarily ignores more heroic varieties of black men, Hogue also points out that the novel is silent

about the thousands of rebellious black women who refused to submit to male authority or to allow themselves to be abused by black men. He offers Janie Starks from Hurston's *Their Eyes Were Watching God* (1937) as an example of more independent women. Indeed, rebellious, aggressive, independent black women have existed throughout American history, but theirs is not the story the text is obliged to tell. Nor is Janie Starks quite the representative example of the rebellious black woman Hogue maintains.

15. See Watkins, "Sexism," p. 35. While Watkins criticizes other black women writers for their negative portraits of black male brutality, he praises Morrison for her "subtle, intelligent prose," which in his view directs our sympathies away from the actual horror of the rape to the swirl of emotions that motivate Cholly's actions.

16. Toni Morrison, *The Bluest Eye* (New York: Washington Square Press, 1970), pp. 128–129; Houston A. Baker Jr., *Blues, Ideology, and Afro-American Literature: A Vernacular Theory* (Chicago: University of Chicago Press, 1984), pp. 177–188.

17. Houston A. Baker Jr., *Workings of the Spirit: The Poetics of Afro-American Women's Writing* (Chicago: University of Chicago Press, 1991), p. 145.

18. Michael Awkward, *Inspiriting Influences: Tradition, Revision, and Afro-American Women's Novels* (New York: Columbia University Press, 1989), pp. 82–83.

19. Zora Neale Hurston, *Their Eyes Were Watching God,* rpt. with foreword by Sherley Anne Williams (Urbana: University of Illinois Press, 1978), p. 41.

20. See Hortense Spillers, "The Politics of Intimacy: A Discussion," in *Sturdy Black Bridges,* pp. 87–106.

21. Hurston, *Their Eyes,* pp. 122–123.

22. Alice Walker, *The Third Life of Grange Copeland* (New York: Harcourt Brace Jovanovich, 1970), p. 94. Later quotations from pp. 102, 103, 107.

23. Toni Morrison, *Song of Solomon* (New York: New American Library, 1977), pp. 217, 218.

24. Richard K. Barksdale, "Castration Symbolism in Recent Black American Fiction," *CLA Journal* 29 (June 1986), 403.

25. Gayl Jones, *Eva's Man* (New York: Random House, 1976), pp. 128–129.

26. My coinage of "dearly beloved blues" was inspired by Alice Walker's short story "Roselily," in which she interweaves the title character's thoughts as she marries a black Muslim with the words of the minister conducting the ceremony. From the details that occupy Roselily's thoughts as the minister speaks—ropes, chains, handcuffs, and "the stiff severity of [the groom's] plain black suit"—we know that this will not be a happy marriage. Also alluding to Walker, Jones calls male-female relationships of

the kind she deals with in *Corregidora* "blues relationships," coming out of a "tradition of 'love and trouble.'" See Walker, "Roselily," in *In Love and Trouble: Stories of Black Women* (New York: Harcourt Brace Jovanovich, 1973), p. 3; "Gayl Jones: An Interview," in Michael S. Harper and Robert Stepto, eds., *Chant of Saints: A Gathering of Afro-American Literature, Art, and Scholarship* (Urbana: University of Illinois Press, 1979), p. 360.

27. Janice Harris, "Gayl Jones' *Corregidora*," *Frontiers* 3 (1981), 2.

28. Gayl Jones, *Corregidora* (Boston: Beacon, 1986), p. 184.

29. Charles H. Rowell, "Interview with Gayl Jones," *Callaloo* 5 (October 1982), p. 45.

30. Melvin Dixon, *Ride Out the Wilderness: Geography and Identity in Afro-American Literature* (Chicago: University of Illinois Press, 1987), p. 112.

31. Barksdale, "Castration Symbolism," p. 402; my emphasis. According to the text, Davis is already dead when Eva dismembers him.

32. Jones, *Corregidora*, p. 3.

33. Dixon, *Ride Out the Wilderness*, p. 117.

34. Ann Allen Shockley, "The Black Lesbian in American Literature," in Barbara Smith, ed., *Home Girls: A Black Feminist Anthology* (New York: Women of Color Press, 1983), p. 89.

35. Bell, "Addison Gayle," pp. 214–215.

36. Rowell, "Interview with Gayl Jones," pp. 46–47.

37. See Reed's novel *Reckless Eyeballing*, among other sources.

38. Clifford Geertz, "Notes on the Balinese Cockfight," in *The Interpretation of Culture* (New York: Basic Books, 1973), p. 443. Geertz writes: "Like any art form . . . the cockfight renders ordinary, everyday experience comprehensible by presenting it in terms of acts and objects which have had their practical consequences removed and been reduced . . . to the level of sheer appearances, where their meaning can be more powerfully articulated and more easily perceived."

39. Janice A. Radway, *Reading the Romance: Women, Patriarchy, and Popular Literature* (Chapel Hill: University of North Carolina Press, 1984), p. 71.

40. Darryl Pinckney, "Black Victims, Black Villains," *New York Review of Books*, January 19, 1987, p. 18.

3. The Occult of True Black Womanhood

1. Bell hooks, *Black Looks: Race and Representation* (Boston: South End Press, 1992), p. 21.

2. Houston A. Baker Jr., *Workings of the Spirit: The Poetics of Afro-American Women's Writing* (Chicago: University of Chicago Press, 1991), pp. 1–2.

3. Michele Wallace, *Invisibility Blues* (New York: Verso, 1990), p. 174.

4. Sherley Anne Williams, in Hurston's *Their Eyes Were Watching God* (Urbana: University of Illinois Press, 1978), p. vi.

5. See e.g. Frances Beal, "Double Jeopardy: To Be Black and Female," in Robin Morgan, ed., *Sisterhood Is Powerful* (New York: Random House, 1970), pp. 340–352; Toni Cade [Bambara], *The Black Woman* (New York: New American Library, 1970); Angela Davis, "Reflections on the Black Woman's Role in the Community of Slaves," *Black Scholar* 3 (1971), 3–15, and *Women, Race and Class* (New York: Random House, 1981); Joyce Ladner, *Tomorrow's Tomorrow: The Black Woman* (New York: Doubleday, 1972); Mary Helen Washington, "Zora Neale Hurston: The Black Woman's Search for Identity," *Black World* (August 1972), 68–75, and "Their Fiction Becomes Our Reality: Black Women Image Makers," *Black World* (August 1974), 10–18; Barbara Christian, *Black Women Novelists: The Development of a Tradition* (Westport, Conn.: Greenwood, 1980) and *Black Feminist Criticism: Perspectives on Black Women Writers* (New York: Pergamon, 1985); Frances Foster, "Changing Concepts of the Black Woman," *Journal of Black Studies* (June 1973), 433–452; Jeanne Noble, *Beautiful, Also, Are the Souls of My Black Sisters* (Englewood Cliffs: Prentice-Hall, 1978); Sharon Harley and Rosalyn Terborg-Penn, eds., *The Afro-American Woman: Struggles and Images* (New York: Kennikat, 1978); Bonnie Thorton Dill, "The Dialectics of Black Womanhood," *Signs* 4 (1979), 543–555, and "Race, Class, and Gender: Prospects for an All-inclusive Sisterhood," *Feminist Studies* 9 (1983), 131–150; Barbara Smith, "Toward a Black Feminist Criticism," *Conditions Two* 1 (1977); Darlene Clark Hine, *When the Truth Is Told: A History of Black Women's Culture and Community in Indiana, 1875–1950* (Indianapolis: National Council of Negro Women, 1981); bell hooks, *Ain't I a Woman: Black Women and Feminism* (Boston: South End Press, 1981); Filomina Chioma Steady, ed., *The Black Woman Cross-Culturally* (Cambridge: Schenkman, 1981); Gloria Hull, Patricia Bell Scott, and Barbara Smith, eds., *All the Women Are White, All the Men Are Black, But Some of Us Are Brave* (Old Westbury, New York: Feminist Press, 1982).

6. For whatever it may suggest about the crisis and the production of the black intellectual, it is interesting to note that the scholarly work of Baker, Gates, and West has been lauded in cover stories and feature articles in such publications as the *New York Times*, the *Boston Globe*, *Newsweek*, and *Time*. I recall seeing only one article on Mary Helen Washington, in the "Learning" section of the Sunday *Boston Globe* (although there may have been others). The article is dominated by a stunning picture of Washington, with a caption describing her as a scholar-teacher who "helps restore sight to the 'darkened eye' of American literary tradition." Despite this fitting and promising caption, the article has remarkably little to say about Washington's actual scholarship and its impact on

American literary studies. See Elizabeth Weld, "The Voice of Black Women," *Boston Globe*, February 14, 1988, pp. 98, 100.

7. Wallace, *Invisibility Blues*, p. 184.

8. Cheryl A. Wall, ed., *Changing Our Own Words: Essays on Criticism, Theory, and Writing by Black Women* (New Brunswick: Rutgers University Press, 1989), pp. 4–5.

9. See Baker, *Workings of the Spirit*, p. 10. Most of the black feminist critics listed by Baker have produced essays and books too numerous to name. In addition to their own writings, several of these scholars have made tremendous contributions to the fields of African American and black feminist literary studies through their editorial work on a number of important projects. See e.g. Trudier Harris and Thadious Davis, eds., *Afro-American Writers from the Harlem Renaissance to 1940, Dictionary of Literary Biography*, vol. 51 (Detroit: Gale Research), and Beacon Press's Black Women Writers Series, ed. Deborah McDowell.

10. For such a review of the critical literature, see Hazel Carby, *Reconstructing Black Womanhood: The Emergence of the Afro-American Woman Novelist* (New York: Oxford University Press, 1987), and Wall's introduction to *Changing Our Own Words*, pp. 1–15.

11. Gayatri Chakravorty Spivak, "In Praise of *Sammy and Rosie Get Laid*," *Critical Quarterly* 31-2 (1989), 80–88.

12. August Meier and Elliot Rudwick, *Black History and the Historical Profession, 1915–1980* (Urbana: University of Illinois Press, 1986), p. 294; Darlene Clark Hine, "The Four Black Historical Movements: A Case for the Teaching of Black History," *Teaching History: A Journal of Methods* 5 (1980), 115, quoted in Meier and Rudwick.

13. Harriet Jacobs, *Incidents in the Life of a Slave Girl, Written by Herself* (1861), ed. Jean Fagan Yellin (Cambridge: Harvard University Press, 1987), p. 246.

14. Gloria Wade-Gayles, *No Crystal Stair: Visions of Race and Sex in Black Women's Fiction* (New York: Pilgrim Press, 1984), pp. 41–42.

15. Gerda Lerna, ed., *Black Women in White America: A Documentary History* (New York: Random House, 1972), pp. xviii, xx.

16. Anna Julia Cooper, *A Voice from the South*, rpt. with introduction by Mary Helen Washington (New York: Oxford University Press, 1988), p. ii.

17. See Charles Nichols, *Many Thousand Gone: The Ex-Slaves' Account of Their Bondage and Freedom* (Bloomington: Indiana University Press, 1963).

18. Stephen Fender, "African Accents, Tall Tales," review of *Was Huck Black?* by Shelley Fisher Fishkin, and *Mark Twain and the Art of the Tall Tale*, by Henry B. Wonham, *Times Literary Supplement*, July 16, 1993, p. 27.

19. Karen J. Winkler, "A Scholar's Provocative Query: Was Huckleberry Finn Black?" *Chronicle of Higher Education*, July 8, 1992, p. A6.

20. David Levering Lewis, "Parallels and Divergences: Assimilationist Strategies of Afro-American and Jewish Elites from 1910 to the Early 1930s," *Journal of American History* 71 (1984), 543–564.

21. Barbara Christian, Ann duCille, Sharon Marcus, Elaine Marks, Nancy K. Miller, Sylvia Schafer, and Joan W. Scott, "Conference Call," *differences* 2 (fall 1990), 61.

22. Elizabeth Abel, "Black Writing, White Reading: Race and the Politics of Feminist Interpretation," *Critical Inquiry* 19 (Spring 1993), 478.

23. Barbara Johnson has called Henry Louis Gates on his repeated use of the term "our own," noting nineteen instances in one essay. She goes on to query his meaning: "Does Gates mean all black people (whatever that might mean)? All Afro-Americans? All scholars of Afro-American literature? All black men? All scholars trained in literary theory who are now interested in the black vernacular?" See Henry Louis Gates Jr., "Canon-Formation and the Afro-American Tradition," and Johnson's response, both in Houston A. Baker Jr. and Patricia Redmond, eds., *Afro-American Literary Studies in the 1990s* (Chicago: University of Chicago Press, 1989), pp. 13–49.

24. For those of us tempted to make common experience the essence of critical interpretation or to view black women's fiction as expressive realism, Belsey's words may be instructive: "The claim that a literary form reflects the world is simply tautological. What is intelligible as realism is the conventional and therefore familiar . . . It is intelligible as 'realistic' precisely because it reproduces what we already seem to know." *Critical Practice* (New York: Routledge, 1980), p. 47.

25. Indira Karamcheti, "Caliban in the Classroom," *Radical Teacher* 44 (Winter 1993), 13–17.

26. Baker, *Workings of the Spirit*, p. 11.

27. Jane Gallop, Marianne Hirsch, and Nancy K. Miller, "Criticizing Feminist Criticism," in Hirsch and Evelyn Fox Keller, eds., *Conflicts in Feminism* (New York: Routledge, 1989), p. 363.

28. Gayatri Chakravorty Spivak, *In Other Worlds: Essays in Cultural Politics* (New York: Routledge, 1988), p. 81.

29. Elizabeth Spelman, *Inessential Woman: Problems of Exclusion in Feminist Thought* (Boston: Beacon Press, 1988), p. 13. Echoing the complaint that women of color have leveled for some time (at least since Sojourner Truth's public query "Ain't I a woman?" first asked more than 140 years ago), Spelman argues that holding their own experiences to be normative, many white feminists historically have given little more than lip service to the significance of race and class in the lives of women.

30. Gallop, Hirsch, and Miller, "Criticizing Feminist Criticism," pp. 363–364.

31. Ibid., p. 358.

32. Jane Gallop, *Around 1981: Academic Feminist Literary Theory* (New York: Routledge, 1992), p. 169.

33. Ibid., p. 170; my emphasis.

34. Quoted in Meier and Rudwick, *Black History*, p. 289.

35. Adrienne Rich, *Of Woman Born: Motherhood as Experience and Institution*, 10th anniversary ed. (New York: Norton, 1986), pp. 254–255.

36. Ibid., p. xxviii.

37. In the anniversary revised edition of *Of Woman Born*, a more reflective Adrienne Rich attempts to adjust her vision in light of 1980s concerns. To her discussion of "my Black mother" she appends a footnote: "The above passage overpersonalizes and does not, it seems to me now, give enough concrete sense of the actual position of the Black domestic worker caring for white children." Even ten years later, Rich has failed to recognize that she is talking about another woman—another woman who is not her black mother but a laborer whose role as mammy is also constructed.

38. Lerner, *Black Women*, pp. xviii, xix; my emphasis.

39. John F. Callahan, *In the African-American Grain: Call-and-Response in Twentieth-Century Black Fiction*, 2nd ed. (Middletown: Wesleyan University Press, 1989), pp. 5, 9. Later quotations from pp. 10, 21, 8.

40. Missy Dehn Kubitschek, *Claiming the Heritage: African-American Women Novelists and History* (Jackson: University Press of Mississippi, 1991), p. xii. Later quotations from p. xxi.

41. In the final moments of her personal preface, we learn that it was actually the survival strategies embedded in black literature that ultimately led Kubitschek to the work of African American women writers. "The stories that constitute African-American literature say that oppression kills and that people survive oppression," she tells us. "Wanting to know more about survival brought me here" (p. xxiii).

42. Baker, *Workings of the Spirit*, pp. 208–209.

43. Mae Henderson, "Commentary on 'There Is No More Beautiful Way: Theory and the Poetics of Afro-American Women's Writing,'" by Houston Baker, in Baker and Patricia Redmond, eds., *Afro-American Literary Studies in the 1990s* (Chicago: University of Chicago Press, 1989), p. 159.

44. Baker, *Workings of the Spirit*, p. 212.

45. Hazel Carby, "The Multicultural Wars," in Gina Dent, ed., *Black Popular Culture* (Seattle: Bay Press, 1992), p. 192.

46. Patricia Sharpe, F. E. Mascia-Lee, and C. B. Cohen, "White Women and Black Men: Different Responses to Reading Black Women's Texts," *College English* 52 (1990), 146.

47. Cherrie Moraga, "Preface," in Moraga and Gloria Anzaldua, eds., *This Bridge Called My Back: Writings by Radical Women of Color* (New York: Women of Color Press, 1981), p. xv.

48. For a report on the conference, see Saidiya Hartman, "The Territory Between Us," *Callaloo* 17.2 (1994), 439–449. It was especially poignant that the opening address was delivered by Lani Guinier. Under a gag order from the Whitehouse, she was prohibited from responding to her critics—from defending her name—while her nomination was pending, despite the opposition's flagrant misrepresentation of her views. Noting that her written work had been repeatedly taken out of context and otherwise distorted, Guinier quipped that her experience gave new meaning to the term "publish or perish": she did both.

4. Discourse and Dat Course

1. See Kobena Mercer, "Black Hair/Style Politics," in Russell Ferguson, Martha Gever, Trinh T. Minh-ha, and Cornel West, eds., *Out There: Marginalization and Contemporary Cultures* (New York and Cambridge: New Museum of Contemporary Art and MIT Press, 1992), pp. 247–264. Mercer writes that "however strongly these styles express a desire to 'return to the roots' among black peoples in the diaspora, in Africa *as it is* they would speak of a 'modern' orientation, a modelling of oneself according to metropolitan images of blackness" (p. 256).

2. See Greg Thomas, "The Black Studies War," *Village Voice*, January 17, 1995, pp. 23–29.

3. See Jerry Adler et al., "African Dreams," *Newsweek*, September 23, 1991, pp. 42–43.

4. Ella Shohat, "Notes on the 'Post-Colonial,'" *Social Text* 31-32 (1992), 101.

5. Indira Karamcheti, "Disciplining Postcoloniality: or, Taking Liberties with Countee Cullen," paper given at the Johns Hopkins University, Baltimore, April 30, 1993.

6. See Paget Henry and Paul Buhle, "Caliban as Deconstructionist: C.L.R. James and Post-Colonial Discourse," in Henry and Buhle, eds., *C.L.R. James's Caribbean* (Durham: Duke University Press, 1992), pp. 111–142; see also Edward Said, *Culture and Imperialism* (New York: Knopf, 1993). Said traces the history of textual or discursive insurrection—what he calls an "oppositional strain"—in the works of a variety of writers who, in one way or another and often in the "master's" own tongue, challenged the colonial order.

7. Anne McClintock, "The Angel of Progress: Pitfalls of the Term 'Post-Colonialism,'" *Social Text* 31-32 (1992), 91–92.

8. Karamcheti, "Disciplining Postcoloniality," pp. 2–3, 4–5.

9. Shohat, "Notes on the 'Post-Colonial,'" p. 108.

10. Cornel West, *Race Matters* (Boston: Beacon Press, 1993), p. 4.

11. See Barbara Ransby, "Afrocentrism, Cultural Nationalism, and the Problem with Essentialist Definitions of Race, Gender, and Sexuality," *Race and Reason* 1 (1994), 31–34.

12. Henry Louis Gates Jr., "Writing 'Race' and the Difference It Makes," in Gates, ed., *"Race," Writing, and Difference* (Chicago: University of Chicago Press, 1985), p. 5; Gayatri Chakravorty Spivak, "Interview with Sneja Gunew," in Sarah Harasym, ed., *The Post-Colonial Critic: Interview, Strategies, Dialogues* (New York: Routledge, 1990), p. 64.

13. There is of course much irony in this nomenclature, since the term "Native American" also invokes the colonizer, Amerigo Vespucci, for whom the Americas are named.

14. As quoted in Thomas, "The Black Studies War," p. 23.

15. Barbara Johnson, "Canon-Formation and the Afro-American Tradition," in Houston A. Baker Jr. and Patricia Redmond, eds., *Afro-American Literary Studies in the 1990s* (Chicago: University of Chicago Press, 1989), p. 42.

16. Said, *Culture and Imperialism*, p. 336.

5. The Blacker the Juice

1. *Newsweek* stated that in 1969 Simpson told a reporter: "my biggest accomplishment is that people look at me like a man first, not a black man." He went on to describe an incident at a wedding where he, his first wife, and a few friends were the only black people in attendance. He overheard a white woman say, "Look, there's O. J. Simpson and some niggers." Simpson told the reporter that he was hurt by the remark, "even though it's what I strive for, to be a man first." See Jonathan Alter, "Black & White & Read All Over," *Newsweek*, August 1, 1994, p. 19.

2. I don't recall that the press picked it up, but it seems noteworthy that Denise Brown's description of Simpson's narrowing, darkening eyes and menacing stare closely resembled what her sister reportedly told the police who responded to the 911 call: "When he gets this crazed, I get scared . . . He gets a very animalistic look in him . . . His eyes are black, just black, I mean cold, like an animal." Nicole's remarks are as quoted in *Spy*, November-December 1995, p. 57.

3. See Vivian B. Martin, "Simpson Trial Offers Lessons in Trans-racial Dialogue," *Hartford Courant*, April 20, 1995, p. A23.

4. "The O. J. Simpson Case: Prominent Blacks Discuss Race, Sex,

Crime, and 'the Case of the Century,'" *Ebony*, September 1994, pp. 29–35, 140–141.

5. Jeffrey Toobin, "Putting It in Black and White," *New Yorker*, July 17, 1995, p. 32.

6. CBS, *American Journal*, July 20, 1995.

7. See *National Enquirer*, July 19, 1994, cover and pp. 36–37. On the cover the trio appears to be in a hot tub; in the inside photo, it looks as if she and her boyfriend are in two baskets of some kind, while a second man is hugging her from behind and cupping her breasts.

8. Richard Hoffer, "Fatal Attraction," *Sports Illustrated*, June 27, 1994, p. 22.

9. John Fiske, *Media Matters: Everyday Culture and Political Change* (Minneapolis: University of Minnesota Press, 1994), pp. 1–2.

10. Time plays tricks with historical memory and makes the immediate seem the most important. Still, in a century that has witnessed the assassination of two presidents, the Holocaust, the Nuremberg trials, extensive racial violence—including the 1963 bombing of a church in which four black girls were killed—I think we must ask what made this particular event the crime and the trial of the century. Why was it so overproduced by the media and so hungrily consumed by the masses?

11. Larry Reibstein and Charles Fleming, "Gorging on the Buffet," *Newsweek*, October 3, 1994, p. 45. The comment is attributed to Andy Friendly, a producer for CNBC. See also "The O. J. Simpson Industry," *Investigative Reports*, A&E, July 21, 1995. Car dealers were also among those who gorged on the buffet. The sale of white Ford Broncos skyrocketed, with one dealer advertising that his Broncos came with air conditioning and orange juice, so that customers could have A.C. and O.J. Among the most offensive of the instabooks is Simpson's own *I Want to Tell You*—a particularly grotesque marketing of the murders, for which Simpson was said to get a million dollars. Simpson's fortune was seriously tapped by the cost of defending himself, but he continued to make money behind bars, signing hundreds of thousands of dollars worth of football cards in addition to the book. Carnival Cruise Lines sponsored an O. J. Simpson cruise, a four-day sail from Los Angeles to Ensenada, Mexico. For fares ranging from $469 to $519, "trial junkies" had the unique opportunity to talk with experts such as law professor Stan Goldman. Simpson's own post-trial video was much less successful, selling only 40,000 copies in the first few months. Calls to A. C. Cowlings's 1–900–"Ask A. C." line cost $2.99 a minute; the venture reportedly took in $300,000 in the first month.

12. Idle speculation of course, but I think it fairly safe to say that if the judge had been a white man, we would not have had the Dancing Itos, an ensemble of five Asian American male dancers, all wearing glasses and

fake beards, who made frequent appearances on the *Tonight Show* throughout the spring of 1995. Indeed, the trial became fodder for comedy on a number of TV programs, including *Saturday Night Live* and the *Tonight Show*. For over a year O.J. jokes were the principal gags around which Jay Leno built his nightly monologues. The Dancing Itos brought down the house each time they appeared, as did a series of skits featuring actors made up to resemble Marcia Clark, Christopher Darden, Robert Shapiro, and Johnnie Cochran in takeoffs on *The Brady Bunch,* complete with Florence Henderson; and *Fiddler on the Roof,* featuring a Shapiro lookalike singing "If O.J. Were a Poor Man." Given the dead bodies and motherless children at the heart of this event, one must be uncomfortable with the urge to turn tragedy into comedy and commodity. Judge Ito himself, however, might tell me to lighten up; he was said to be delighted with the dancers and comedy routines. In April 1995, he invited Leno to entertain the sequestered jurors.

13. See Mary Ann Doane, "Dark Continents: Epistemologies of Racial and Sexual Difference in Psychoanalysis and the Cinema," in her *Femmes Fatales: Feminism, Film Theory, Psychoanalysis* (New York: Routledge, 1991), p. 228.

14. Faye D. Resnick, with Mike Walker, *Nicole Brown Simpson: The Private Diary of a Life Interrupted* (Beverly Hills: Dove Books, 1994). Resnick claims two motives for writing the book: a need to tell Nicole's story and a hope that the story might inspire women "trapped in corrosive and humiliating relationships like the one Nicole did not survive" to "seek help in escaping the cycle of violence" (p. xii). A caption on the dust jacket says that a portion of the proceeds from the book will go into a trust fund for Nicole's children. These are the same children who—wanting to know the truth about their mother—may some day turn to Resnick's book and be confronted with such details as their mother's fondness for black men and her penchant for oral sex.

15. Race, one might argue, was a factor in the rape trial of William Kennedy Smith, but whiteness and its privileges are so normative, so much taken for granted, that the accused's racial identity was never a matter open to public or press consideration, much less debate. As one black theorist points out: "In a racially imperialist nation such as ours, it is the dominant race that reserves for itself the luxury of dismissing racial identity while the oppressed race is made daily aware of their racial identity." See bell hooks, *Ain't I a Woman* (Boston: South End Press, 1981), p. 138.

16. The *New York Times* describes Johnnie Cochran as Los Angeles's most prominent black attorney, but even before the trial made his name a household word, Cochran's fame was hardly limited to one city. See

Bella Stumbo, "Bobby and O.J. and Howard and Michael and Johnnie and Liz," *New York Times Magazine*, September 11, 1994, p. 78. The article is an inside look at "L.A.'s exclusive club of celebrity lawyers." The full-page color portrait of Robert Shapiro that accompanies the article brought the onetime head of the Simpson dream team considerable criticism (and perhaps a few more clients) for what some lawyers felt was inappropriate showmanship. Similar criticisms were made of Cochran for his nightly press conferences and autograph signings on the steps of the courthouse.

17. See sidebar, "'Not for the Timid': Johnnie Cochran defends his closing argument," *Newsweek*, October 9, 1995, p. 31.

18. Robert Shapiro to Barbara Walters on an ABC *Special Report*, October 3, 1995. Shapiro also told Walters that he will never again work with Johnnie Cochran or speak to F. Lee Bailey.

19. Larry Reibstein, Mark Miller, and Donna Foote, "Playing the Race Card," *Newsweek*, February 20, 1995, p. 48.

20. In an interview that aired on *48 Hours*, September 7, 1995, Cochran described himself as "somewhat regretful" about implying that Darden was added to the prosecution team only because of the makeup of the jury. He went on to say that he didn't want to aid the system by pitting two black men against each other.

21. Fiske, *Media Matters*, p. xxv.

22. On this point see also Elly Bulkin and Becky W. Thompson, "The Spectacle of Race in the O. J. Simpson Case," *Sojourner,* September 1994, pp. 9–11; Wendy Kozol, "Fracturing Domesticity: Media, Nationalism, and the Question of Feminist Influence," *Signs* 20 (Spring 1995), 646–667; and "The World According to Toni Morrison," *Essence,* May 1995, pp. 224, 273–275, 280. Morrison's remarks are especially provocative: "I'm also concerned about the number of national issues that are being played out with Black men: sexual harassment, police brutality, rape, wife battering, murder. All of these issues are being worked out in television epics, and so a legal case becomes a case of national anxiety. People used to make up epics to describe a war or a romance or a tragedy. Today, in the absence of Homer, we have these long, sustained media spectacles, and we frequently cast Black men in the lead roles because the theatricality and the emotional baggage are more intense" (p. 274).

23. See K. Anthony Appiah, "'No Bad Nigger': Blacks as the Ethical Principle in the Movies," in Marjorie Garber, Jann Matlock, and Rebecca L. Walkowitz, eds., *Media Spectacles* (New York: Routledge, 1993), p. 83. For all the dramatic roles he has played, Poitier, the first African American male actor to win an Oscar, received that award for *Lilies of the Field* (1963), in which he plays a handyman, harmless enough for the company of nuns.

24. *Newsweek,* June 27, 1994, p. 18. Terms like "self-ingratiating" and "self-effacing" were frequently used to describe Simpson. In *Sports Illustrated:* "Simpson was so self-effacing and eager to please that he was deemed unthreatening to whites and thus became the first black athlete to be embraced as an endorser of products not marketed solely to blacks." See Hoffer, "Fatal Attraction," p. 20.

25. See James Gaines, "To Our Readers," *Time,* July 4, 1994, p. 4.

26. *Newsweek*'s bold red caption for its June 27 issue reads: TRAIL OF BLOOD.

27. Jeffrey Klein, "Crime and Punishment," *Mother Jones,* September–October 1994, p. 3. I may do Klein a disservice in taking his comments out of context: "When a hero collided with his dark side, the ancient Greeks called it tragic fate," he writes. "We no longer embrace this concept because it diminishes our sense of free will. Yet we fear the collective will (government, religion) as oppressive, and individual wills as predatory. How then should we govern our natures?"

28. Kozol, "Fracturing Domesticity," pp. 658–659.

29. The cover story in *People,* August 1, 1994, "Nicole Simpson and Ronald Goldman: The Forgotten Victims," was one such self-conscious attempt to remember, if not honor, the dead.

30. The absence is particularly ironic since the article on domestic violence is followed by a sidebar in which the author notes the media's inattention to the victims. (See Margaret Carlson, "The Victim, You Say?" *Time,* July 4, 1994, p. 27.) *Newsweek* also had a cover story on domestic violence in its July 4 issue. Nicole Simpson is pictured on the cover, and one article about the case does include a transcript of her 911 call, but again the story about spousal abuse is not her story. Although her death is clearly the occasion for the story, she in fact merits only a paragraph in an eight-page article. Interestingly enough, however, in September 1994, Johnnie Cochran blasted *Newsweek* for its reporting of Simpson's alleged domestic discord. According to Cochran, the accusations of wife battery are offensive to the family of a man who has lived "an exemplary life."

31. Sara Rimer, "Nicole Simpson: Private Pain Amid Life in the Public Eye," *New York Times,* June 23, 1994, pp. A1, A20.

32. Wahneema Lubiano, "Black Ladies, Welfare Queens, and State Minstrels: Ideological War by Narrative Means," in Toni Morrison, ed., *Race-ing Justice, En-gendering Power: Essays on Anita Hill, Clarence Thomas, and the Construction of Social Reality* (New York: Pantheon, 1992), p. 324.

33. Nancy Gibbs, "End of the Run," *Time,* July 4, 1994, pp. 29–30.

34. Larry Reibstein et al., "Just an All-American," *Newsweek,* July 24, 1995, p. 58.

35. Paul O'Donnell with Patricia King, "'Looking Forward to Being

Nicole,'" *Newsweek,* August 29, 1994, pp. 46–47; the quoted remarks are those of Patricia Rose, reportedly a friend of Nicole's. (This article is part of an eight-page "Special Report," the overall title for which is "The Double Life of O. J. Simpson." See next note.)

36. Evan Thomas, "Special Report: Day and Night, the Double Life of O. J. Simpson," *Newsweek,* August 29, 1994, p. 43; later quotations from p. 46.

37. Simpson reportedly played golf with Bill Clinton at the Del Mar country club only months before the murders.

38. Thomas, "Day and Night," p. 49.

39. Gibbs, "End of the Run," p. 32.

40. Thomas, "Day and Night," pp. 45, 49, 43.

41. On July 12, 1995, Darden attempted to question Robert Heidstra, a white defense witness, about statements made to friends that he had heard two men quarreling on the night of the murders, one who sounded like a young white man and the other who sounded like an older black man. Darden's question drew an angry objection from Cochran, that both the prosecutor and the question were racist. Darden countered that he was merely quoting witnesses; any racism embedded in the question was theirs, not his. He added that such charges of racism (of Uncle Tomism) from Cochran had caused many problems for him and his family. Darden's question was, in my layperson's opinion, legally appropriate, since he was referring to sworn statements from several individuals about what the witness had said to them. Cochran's strategic objection, however, successfully diverted attention away from his client and onto the volatile issue of racism.

42. *Newsweek,* August 29, 1994, p. 48.

43. David H. Hackworth and Peter Annin, "The Suspect Speaks Out," *Newsweek,* July 3, 1995, p. 23.

44. David H. Hackworth, "Talking 'Soldier to Soldier' Behind Bars," *Newsweek,* July 3, 1995, p. 28.

45. On October 25, 1994, Susan Smith of Union, South Carolina, reported that her two young sons had been abducted by a black male carjacker. Nine days and a massive manhunt later, she confessed to having driven her Mazda into a lake with her children still strapped in their carseats inside. She was tried, convicted, and sentenced to life in prison. Almost exactly five years earlier in October 1989, Charles Stuart shot and killed his pregnant wife, telling police that they had been attacked by a black man as they were leaving a childbirth class in Boston.

46. "Letters," *Newsweek,* July 10, 1995, p. 10.

47. In the fall of 1994, the California legislature passed the "check-book" journalism law prohibiting witnesses to crimes from selling their

stories to the media before giving sworn testimony in court. The law, a direct result of the Simpson case, was ruled unconstitutional in August 1995.

48. See "The 'Dream Team' Behind Our O.J. Coverage," *Newsweek*, October 9, 1992, p. 2.

49. See "To Our Readers," *Time*, October 16, 1995, p. 4.

50. Gibbs, "End of the Run," p. 30.

51. In this personal narrative, Harrison tells us that she assumed Simpson's guilt on the evidence available to her. She does not tell us what that evidence is, but it seems in some measure to be black maleness itself and her own experience with it: her lover is a black man. "When I heard O. J. Simpson's voice on the 911 tapes I heard my lover's voice," she writes, "the color of which, dark mahogany, has been my delight, a melody of arousal. Deep in his throat, clotted with loathing, it was . . . I have heard my lover's voice sound like that. My blood, which dances in my veins when he loves me, turns to ice . . ." (both sets of ellipses are in the original text). Are we to extrapolate from this exotic nonsense that black men not only look alike but sound and act alike as well? If we follow Harrison's train of thought to its logical terminus, she, like Nicole Simpson, is a dead woman. But, lest we think the author a racist, she prefaces her treatise on black male voices of violence by informing us that she has never understood enmity based on color and has herself always been exempt from it. In fact, as a child she used to "toddle up to black strangers on the bus, caress their skin, and tell them how beautiful they were." See Harrison, "Killing Love," *Mother Jones*, October 1994, pp. 52–55.

52. Jeffrey Klein, "Crime and Punishment," *Mother Jones*, October 1994, p. 3.

53. Thomas, "Day and Night," pp. 42–43, 45–46.

54. Bill Turque, Andrew Murr, Mark Miller, et al., "He Could Run . . . But He Couldn't Hide," *Newsweek*, June 27, 1994, p. 18.

55. Jonathan Alter, "White and Blue," *Newsweek*, October 16, 1995, p. 66.

56. John McCormick, Mark Starr, Vern Smith, and Howard Fineman, "The Reaction: Whites v. Blacks," *Newsweek*, October 16, 1995, p. 35.

57. With cameras strategically positioned in what they defined as black and white enclaves—churches, barbershops, and beauty salons, on the one hand, and Starbucks and the Juice Club, on the other—the media set out to capture the prescribed responses to the verdict: glee from blacks and gloom from whites. Little or no forum was given either to the millions of blacks who found the evidence of guilt compelling and the verdict deeply disturbing or to the millions of whites who either believed Simpson was framed or who, like the jury, at least found grounds for reason-

able doubt. Nor was any forum afforded the millions of "other" Americans who seem not to count at all in what was constructed as a black and white drama.

58. Consider how often we were told by the likes of *Newsweek* and *Time* and by commentators from Peter Jennings to Geraldo Rivera that the jurors were "not educated," "not rocket scientists," "not Einsteins," "mostly working class," "often bored and sometimes confused by scientific evidence." In a reflective article on the jury, *Newsweek* noted that only two of the jurors graduated from college and concluded that Judge Ito "guaranteed a low education level by automatically rejecting anyone who read a newspaper during jury selection." See Mark Miller, Donna Foote, et al., "How the Jury Saw It," *Newsweek,* October 16, 1995, p. 39.

59. Howard Chua-Eoan and Elizabeth Gleick, "Making the Case," *Time,* pp. 55–56.

60. The Judge Ito Jell-O mold was one of numerous items sold by vendors on the sidewalks outside the courthouse. Several members of the media boast of having them, including CNBC's Sheila Stainback and the Associated Press's Linda Deutsch.

Epilogue

1. See Cornel West, *Race Matters* (Boston: Beacon, 1993).

2. Newt Gingrich, *To Renew America* (New York: HarperCollins, 1995), p. 41.

Index

Abel, Elizabeth, 93
Abuse: physical and sexual, 14, 66, 70, 72, 73, 74, 77, 117, 138, 145, 147–148, 176–177n7; psychic, 117, 119. *See also* Rape; Simpson, Nicole Brown: spousal abuse of; Simpson case: domestic violence as issue in; Violence
Academy/academia, 7, 81, 124, 130, 131: black women in, 81, 83, 93, 95, 97–98, 118–119; white women in, 100, 103, 104, 105, 114, 117; Afrocentrism and, 122, 127, 128; Anglo-American, 128; postcolonial scholars in, 129, 131. *See also* Scholars; Women's studies
Affirmative action, 2, 129, 172
Africa/Africans, 3, 4, 120, 121, 127, 128
African American(s), 4, 5, 6, 110, 169; gender relations among, 60, 61; studies, 84, 88, 89, 93, 95, 96, 119, 122, 126, 127, 134, 135; culture, 90, 91; discourse, 96, 135. *See also Black listings*
African Americanism, 112, 123
Afrocentrism, 7, 121, 122, 131–132, 135; academic, 123, 127, 128; postcolonialism and, 123, 125, 126, 127, 128; cultural, 126; defined, 128; empowerment through, 128; methodology, 132–133; essentialism of, 134; narrative of, 134

Aiken, Kimberly, 27
Akbar, Na'im, 128, 184n68
Alexander, Elizabeth, 116
Allen, Marcus, 141
Alterity, 129; commodification of, 7, 41; of black women, 56, 81, 82, 102, 114; ethnic, 56; racial, 56
Althusser, Louis, 143
American Indians, 129–130
Americanism, 7
American Toy Fair, 31
American Tragedy, An (Dreiser), 152
Ammons, Elizabeth, 94
Andrews, William L., 93–94
Angelou, Maya, 86
Anglo-Americanism, 120
Anglocentrism, 117, 134
Appiah, Kwame Anthony, 124, 149
Around 1981: Academic Feminist Literary Theory (Gallop), 101
Asante, Molefi Kete, 122, 123, 127, 132, 134
Asia/Asian Americans, 2, 5, 9, 32, 125, 166
Autobiography of Miss Jane Pittman, The (Gaines), 66, 67
Awkward, Michael, 68–69

Baker, Houston, 67, 68–69, 83, 85, 86, 98, 113–116, 117, 119, 132, 133
Bambara, Toni Cade, 86, 89, 118

Madison Avenue Barbie, 18–19
Madonna, 18, 22
Malcolm X, 170; film, 52
Many Thousand Gone: The Ex-Slaves' Account of Their Bondage and Freedom (Nichols), 90
Marriage, 69, 70–71, 73
Marshall, Paule, 85, 86
Masculinism, 7, 62, 64, 67, 68, 80, 87, 93, 114
Mason, Perry, television character, 11, 13, 165, 166
Mattel, Inc., 17, 27, 31, 52; ethnic Barbie dolls, 2, 30–31, 34–35, 36, 38, 42–43, 44–45; black Barbie dolls, 16, 34, 36; self-image of children and, 17–18; marketing and sales, 18, 20, 21–22, 31, 33, 35, 36–37, 39, 41–42, 43, 45, 48, 50, 54–55; sexuality of Barbie and, 19, 20; black dolls, 33–34, 49; competition, 34, 35–36; ethnic dolls, 36–37, 38, 42–43, 48, 50–51, 54, 56; Ken doll controversy, 39–41. *See also* Barbie dolls; Shani dolls
McAdoo, Harriet Pipes, 46
McClintock, Anne, 126
McDowell, Deborah, 61, 86, 100–101, 102, 105, 107
McKay, Claude, 125
McKay, Nellie, 86
McVeigh, Timothy, 158, 159, 173
Media, 7, 27, 143, 190n6; racism in, 118, 122–123, 158, 161. *See also* Simpson case: media coverage of
Mercer, Kobena, 53, 194n1
Miller, Nancy, 102, 119
Miss America Pageant, 21, 26, 27, 181n32
Miss Universe contest, 26, 27
Mitchell, Deborah, 37, 48–50
Moraga, Cherrie, 118
Morrison, Toni, 61, 65, 67–68, 69, 71–72, 79, 85, 86, 93, 95, 114, 117, 188n15, 198n22
Mossell, Mrs. N. F., 90
Motherhood, 106–107
Mother Jones, 136, 162

Moynihan Report, 184n68
Multiculturalism, 4–5, 7, 82, 88–89, 132; in toy industry, 36, 37, 38, 42, 45; capitalism and, 42; black literature and, 91; Afrocentrism and, 122, 123. *See also* Barbie dolls: multicultural versions of

Narrative: of beauty, 18, 19, 20, 22; of success, 18, 19; of sex, 20–21; male/female, 114; resistance, 123, 126, 127; Afrocentrism and, 134; racial, 149, 163
Native Son (Wright), 73, 80
Neufield, Peter, 166, 167
Newsweek magazine: coverage of Simpson case, 137, 149, 154, 156, 158, 159–161, 163, 164, 202n58; portrayal of Timothy McVeigh, 158, 159; on Rodney King trial, 163
Nichols, Charles, 90
Nichter, Mimi, 25
Nicole Brown Simpson: The Private Diary of a Life Interrupted (Resnick), 145
Nicole Brown Simpson Foundation, 151
"Nigger," 6–7, 9, 109, 112, 136, 137; use of word in Simpson case, 137, 145, 147
Nixon, Richard, 143, 170
Noble, Jeanne, 85, 89
Notes on the State of Virginia (Jefferson), 3, 4

Of Love and Dust (Gaines), 66, 67
Of Woman Born: Motherhood as Experience and Institution (Rich), 106
O.J. Simpson Super Pro doll, 136
Oklahoma City bombing, 158, 159, 171
Olmec Toys, 182n46
O'Sickey, Ingeborg Majer, 21
Other/otherness, 82, 116, 119, 131, 172, 173; black women as, 81, 82, 102, 114; black, 108, 123; foreign, 125, 126, 167

Patriarchy, 22, 64, 73, 76, 79, 106, 128; white, 66, 71; black, 71